Personal Financial Planning and Investment Pocket Guide

Joel G. Siegel, Ph.D., CPA

Jae K. Shim, Ph.D.

McGraw-Hill Publishing Company
New York   St. Louis   San Francisco   Auckland   Bogotá
Caracas   Colorado Springs   Hamburg   Lisbon
London   Madrid   Mexico   Milan   Montreal
New Delhi   Oklahoma City   Panama   Paris
San Juan   São Paulo   Singapore
Sydney   Tokyo   Toronto

Library of Congress Cataloging-in-Publication Data

Siegel, Joel G.
    Personal financial planning and investment pocket guide / Joel G.
Siegel, Jae K. Shim.
        p.   cm.
    Includes index.
    ISBN 0-07-057538-X :
    1. Finance, Personal.   2. Investments.   I. Shim, Jae K.
II. Title.
HG179.S47 1989
322.024—dc19   88-29395
                                                                     CIP

1234567890   KGP/KGP   8954321098

ISBN 0-07-057538-X

*The editors for this book were Martha Jewett and Barbara Toniolo, the
designer was Naomi Auerbach, and the production supervisor was Richard
A. Ausburn. It was set in Primer by TCSystems, Inc.*

Printed and bound by Kingsport Press

*For more information about other McGraw-Hill materials, call
1-800-2-MCGRAW in the United States. In other countries, call
your nearest McGraw-Hill office.*

To

Contents

Part 2. Putting Your Money to Work

5. Should You Invest in Common Stock?   77

6. Should You Invest in Fixed Income
   Securities?   123

Preface

This handy reference guide and problem solver applies the basic concepts and techniques of personal financial planning and investing to solving everyday financial problems. It is filled with easy-to-follow examples from daily life which show you step by step what has to be done to maximize your financial well-being.

Part 1 deals with the basics of personal financial planning. Chapter 1 shows you how to prepare a budget to determine what you are worth and to help with planning the future. In Chapter 2, computations involving the time value of money are presented, including determining what an investment today will give you in the future (e.g., retirement plan), how much you will have to pay annually on a loan, and how many years will be needed before you can buy a home. The information needed for investing is covered in Chapter 3. The various types of assets you may own and the proper mix are clearly presented. There is always a trade-off between risk and return, which is the subject of Chapter 4. As the saying goes, "You do not get something for nothing." The ways to measure return are presented. Types of risk are identified and ways to curtail them are given.

In Part 2, we put your money to work. Chapter 5 discusses whether you should invest in common stock and, if so, how much.

It depends on many factors and your personal circumstances! What are the characteristics of fixed income securities? Are they for you? Do you want current fixed income more than possible appreciation in value? These questions and more are answered in Chapter 6. Many of us want professionals to manage our money. We desire a diversified portfolio of investments. Thus, what we need to know about mutual funds can be found in Chapter 7.

Part 3 deals with managing a lifetime of financial security. Chapter 8 reviews the financial considerations in buying a home—what price to pay, what you can afford, and what financing source should be used. Chapter 9 describes how to take on and manage debt: what you should know about taking on credit, the real cost of the financing, and whether you should pay off a loan early. After finishing Chapter 10, you will know how to save to meet college costs for your children as well as how to determine what these costs will be. You want to have enough money to live comfortably after retirement. Well, Chapter 11 shows how to accomplish this. It explains how to estimate your retirement needs, pick the "right" pension plan, and determine how much to contribute each year.

The content of the book is clear, concise, and to the point. It contains a host of illustrations, checklists, guidelines, step-by-step instructions, practical applications, and "how-to's" for dealing with those important personal financial planning and investment decisions we all come across daily.

Acknowledgments

We wish to express our appreciation to Martha Jewett for her exceptional editorial guidance and assistance for this project. She was the one who originally came up with the idea and framework for this book. Martha carefully guided us through this undertaking. Her input and efforts are well appreciated. She deserves a great deal of credit for imagination, intellectual ability, and hard work. We feel deeply indebted to her. Special thanks also go to Barbara B. Toniolo, who did a superb job during the production/editorial stage.

Part 1

The ABCs of Personal Financial Planning

1

Personal Financial Statements and Budgeting

What is your net worth? You will learn how to determine it in this chapter. The greater your net worth is, the better the standard of living you will enjoy and the earlier you can retire. A personal financial statement will help you in evaluating your money habits.

A personal financial statement is like a map: it shows your present financial status, reveals where your money is going, and guides you in later financial decisions. Also helpful in planning finances is preparation of a budget showing sources of income and types of expenditures.

How Much Are You Worth?

By preparing a personal balance sheet, you can see how much you own (assets) and owe (liabilities). The difference between assets and liabilities represents net worth. The balance sheet shows the status of your financial position and whether any changes are needed. It may help you answer many questions, such as whether to obtain additional financing, how much insurance you need, what your potential estate is for planning purposes, whether you can buy a house, how much money is available for investments, when you can retire, and what funds are available for the education of children.

Try to maximize your net worth by concentrating on assets and controlling liabilities. Be careful how you finance assets. For example, avoid financing long-term assets with short-term debt.

Use the same criterion every year as a basis for valuing assets and liabilities. For example, if you value your house using recent area sales, do the same next year.

You can compare your personal balance sheet with those of others in your age group or professional category to see how you stack up against your peers.

An abbreviated personal balance sheet would include the following:

Assets

- Liquid assets (e.g., cash and marketable securities)
- Loan assets (e.g., certificates of deposit, bonds)
- Owned assets (e.g., stocks, stock mutual funds, real estate, gold)
- Personal assets (e.g., auto, jewelry)
- Deferred assets (e.g., pension plan, insurance annuities, deferred compensation, trusts and inheritances)

Liabilities

- Short-term debt (e.g., credit cards)
- Intermediate-term debt (e.g., notes, loans)
- Long-term debt (e.g., mortgage)

Net worth = Assets − Liabilities

Your Assets

Assets should be listed in the order of liquidity at current market values. The most liquid assets are cash and marketable securities. Liquid assets can be sold quickly without loss of principal (e.g., money market fund). Assets may be short-term, intermediate-term, or long-term, depending on the maturity date.

Some assets have appreciation potential (e.g., real estate, stocks). Personal assets often depreciate (e.g., automobile, furniture). Deferred assets include retirement plans, trusts, and inheritances that are inaccessible and will be reduced by taxes.

If assets are jointly owned, only your interest as beneficial owner should be included. A listing of assets may take the following form:

Asset   *Description*   *Carrying Value*   *Percent of Total Assets*

How should assets be valued? There are certain guidelines used to derive value, depending on the type of asset. Your assets might include:

- Amount of money in bank savings and checking accounts
- Cash surrender value of life insurance
- United States Savings Bonds at current market price
- Amount you could withdraw today from your profit sharing and retirement program
- Annuities at accumulated current value
- Market value of stocks and bonds (e.g., quoted market price on the exchange, bid price for an over-the-counter security)
- Net asset value of mutual fund shares
- Market value of other investments (e.g., mortgages given to others)

- Current offering price for unit trusts
- Market value of real estate owned, including your house
- Price you could receive for your car or boat (e.g., trade-in value)
- Market value of household items (e.g., furniture, appliances), determined by what you could get for them if you sold them (**Rule of Thumb:** Value household items at 5 percent of the value of the home.)
- Market value of pesonal items (e.g., jewelry, clothing) (**Rule of Thumb:** Jewelry can be valued at 30 percent of the purchase price.)
- Appraised value for collectibles
- Price to be obtained if you sold your investment in an unincorporated business
- Receivables due you from others

EXAMPLE 1.1

You agree to give a mortgage on the house you are selling. You will receive $10,000 each year for 10 years. The interest rate is 10 percent. The present value of the stream of mortgage payments is determined using Table 2.4, "Present Value of Annuity of $1," as follows:

$10,000 × 6.14457 = $61,446

Note: Business interests that represent a large part of total assets should be shown separately from other investments.

Questions You Should Ask about Your Assets

- Are most assets concentrated in one category? (This is not desirable since it lacks diversification.)

- Which of the assets are not liquid, and what do they amount to?
- What is the balance between liquid and nonliquid investments?
- Are your investments resulting in tax benefits or problems?
- What is the fair market value of your assets and how does that differ from your initial cost and book value (initial cost less accumulated depreciation)?
- Which assets are most risky?
- What amount of your assets can be used to meet impending obligations?

Your Liabilities

What about what you owe? Liabilities should be shown at estimated current amounts by order of maturity. Categorize liabilities by final payment date. Bills due within one year (e.g., credit cards) are short-term debt, loans due in between one to five years (e.g., auto and consumer loans) are intermediate-term debt, and debts due in more than five years (e.g., mortgage obligations) are long-term debt.

Liabilities include:

- Amounts owed on the mortgage on the house
- Amounts owed for taxes that have not been withheld
- Funds set aside and earmarked for college

Questions to Be Asked about Your Debt

- Are you debt averse or prone?
- Which assets are being financed by debt?
- What is the interest rate on the debt?

- What is the maturity of debt and repayment schedule?
- What are the sources of repaying the debt (e.g., salary, taking out new loans to pay off old loans, selling assets)?
- What has been the trend in your debt position?

Figure 1.1 shows an illustrative balance sheet.

Recommendation: Compute your ratio of total debt to total assets to determine how much of the assets is financed by debt.

EXAMPLE 1.2

Total debt equals $100,000 and total assets are $200,000. The debt ratio equals:

$$\frac{\text{Total debt}}{\text{Total assets}} = \frac{\$100,000}{\$200,000} = .50$$

For each $1 in assets you have $.50 in debt.

Rule of Thumb: Your debt as a percentage of your total assets should generally be less than 50 percent. If, however, your job position is unstable, the debt percentage should be lower, approximating no more than 25 percent.

Your Net Savings

Net savings equals total income less total expenses. You can prepare an income statement showing your income and expenses. This reveals your economic health and indicates if there is excess discretionary income to save. Looking at the relationship between expenses and income may give you ideas on ways to readjust expenses.

Income sources have to be considered to determine future

MR. JACK SMITH
BALANCE SHEET
DECEMBER 31, 19X9

ASSETS
Liquid

Cash	$ 4,000	
Money market fund	25,000	
Marketable securities	30,000	
Mutual fund	14,000	
Cash surrender value of life insurance	6,000	
Total liquid assets		$79,000

Nonliquid

Long-term investments	$50,000	
Real estate	150,000	
Automobile	10,000	
Personal property	25,000	
Retirement funds	40,000	
Total nonliquid assets		275,000
Total assets		$354,000

LIABILITIES
Short-term

Accounts and bills due	$ 1,000	
Credit card	2,500	
Total short-term liabilities		$ 3,500

Long-term

Mortgage payable	$80,000	
Auto loan	4,000	
Bank loan	3,000	
Total long-term liabilities		87,000
Total liabilities		$90,500
Net worth		$263,500

Figure 1.1 Illustrative balance sheet.

stability and recurrence possibilities. Potential for growth in income may also be revealed. Some sources of income are salaries, interest and dividends, gifts, and pensions. Living expenses are also itemized to see if any category is unusually high, and why. Are your spending habits excessive, and in what areas?

Some Expense Considerations

Managing expenses well has a lot to do with how much you know about your expenses. Therefore, you need answers to the following questions:

- Which expenses are fixed and which variable? Fixed expenses are the same each month (e.g., insurance), and are typically provided by written agreement. Variable expenses may fluctuate each month (e.g., transportation, food).
- What amount of each expense is discretionary?
- Which expenses are excessive, based on your goals?
- Which expenses can be eliminated if costs have to be cut? Recurring expenses (e.g., rent) may not be easily reduced. Nonrecurring expenses (e.g., entertainment and recreation) may be reduced, if necessary.

    Recommendation: Use an Expense Record Book to record expenses. A looseleaf binder will suffice.

An abbreviated income statement should include the following elements:

Income
- Fully taxable income (e.g., salaries, interest, dividends, gains on sale of securities)
- Tax-sheltered income (e.g., Social Security benefits)

- Tax-exempt bond interest
- Retirement plan earnings
- Disability benefits
- Gifts and inheritances

Expenses

- Recurring expenses (e.g., mortgage interest, rent, telephone, electric, insurance)
- Nonrecurring expenses (e.g., food, repairs, transportation, recreation, education, clothing)
- Taxes and tax-sheltered expenses (e.g., taxes, losses on sale of securities, business expenses, health insurance, medical expenses, alimony, donation, child-care costs, home improvements)

    Net Savings = Total income − Total expenses

A sample income statement is given in Figure 1.2.

Figure 1.3 shows the format of illustrative financial statements prepared by Bank of America for distribution to consumers.

How Does Your Budget Look?

You should prepare a budget of the different sources of income (e.g., salary, investment income, pensions) and itemize expenses by category. The preparation of a budget will show how you manage cash flow. A money plan enables you to direct dollars where they are needed most.

Budgeting is best done on a monthly basis, since timely figures are needed to monitor the situation and take timely action. You are able to evaluate your estimated cash balance at the end of each

MR. AND MRS. TOM JONES
INCOME STATEMENT
FOR THE YEAR ENDING DECEMBER 31, 19X8

INCOME

Salary, commission, bonus	$75,000	
Self-employment income (net)	20,000	
Interest	2,000	
Dividends	4,000	
Gain on sale of securities	4,000	
Rental, royalty, and partnership income	5,000	
Pensions, social security	10,000	
Total Income		$120,000

EXPENSES

FIXED EXPENSES

Insurance	$3,000	
Housing (mortgage, rent)	12,000	
Real estate taxes	4,000	
Utilities	2,000	
Medical	2,000	
Groceries	6,000	
Transportation (commuting)	1,000	
Repayment of debt	3,000	
Income taxes	5,000	
Contribution to pension plan	—	
Total fixed expenses		38,000

DISCRETIONARY EXPENSES

Clothing and cleaning	$2,000
Personal care	1,000
Restaurants	5,000
Entertainment/recreation	3,000
Vacation/travel	4,000
Education	3,000
Charities and gifts	1,000

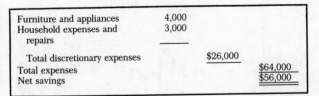

Furniture and appliances	4,000		
Household expenses and repairs	3,000		
	———		
Total discretionary expenses		$26,000	
Total expenses			$64,000
Net savings			$56,000

Figure 1.2 Illustrative income statement.

period (e.g., month, quarter, year). Based on the budget, you can find out what sources of income may be increased to improve the cash balance. You may decide that certain costs have to be cut because of forecasted cash problems. You can separate necessities from luxury expenditures to see which costs you can do without. You can identify which expenses are tax-deductible and which are not. More emphasis should be given to tax-deductible expenses, to obtain tax savings.

An important aspect in budgeting is the control of personal credit. The use of credit should be minimized because of the high financing cost.

EXAMPLE 1.3

You incur a tax-deductible expense (e.g., interest on a mortgage) of $4000. If you are in the 28 percent tax bracket, your after-tax cost is $2880 ($4000 × .72). The remaining $1120 is in effect subsidized by the government because it represents a tax savings.

The Advantages of Budgeting

The use of budgeting will greatly enhance your planning ability.

- It aids in meeting personal goals and planning expenditures.

Balance Sheet

_____ 19___

ASSETS Everything you own that has cash value.

CASH Money you have on hand. Includes cash at home, today's checking and savings account balances. $_____

TIME DEPOSITS Funds deposited for a specified period of time—in a certificate of deposit (CD), for example. $_____

STOCKS, BONDS, OTHER SECURITIES U.S. Savings Bonds, Treasury issues, other money market and stock market investments. Check your records for documentation of current holdings. Current market value for some types of securities may be found in newspaper financial pages; for others, contact your broker. $_____

LIFE INSURANCE CASH SURRENDER VALUE Investment or equity built up in your life insurance policy, *not* the face value. Find the cash surrender value from the chart on your policy. $_____

ACCOUNTS RECEIVABLE Money owed to you for goods and services. Check your files for items outstanding. $_____

NOTES RECEIVABLE Money owed to you and documented by promissory notes. Check your records for the balance of any note due you. $_____

REBATES, REFUNDS Money owed to you for refundable deposits, sales or tax refunds, or rebates. Check your files for receipts and your most recent federal income tax form. $_____

AUTOS, OTHER VEHICLES Trucks, trailers, campers, motorcycles, boats, and airplanes. Vehicle dealers and some libraries carry special price books for new and used automobiles. If no published information is available, dealers may be able to estimate the current market value. $_____

LIABILITIES What you owe; your debts.

ACCOUNTS PAYABLE Total balance of what you owe today on bills for goods and services (such as doctor bills) and credit card and charge accounts. A credit card company or store usually lists your account's total balance due on the monthly statement mailed to you. If you don't have these records, contact the credit department of firms where you have accounts. $_____

CONTRACTS PAYABLE Total remaining balance on installment credit contracts for goods such as a car, furniture, appliances, or services of someone working for you under contract. To figure the total amount due, multiply your monthly payment by the number of months remaining on the contract. $_____

NOTES PAYABLE Total balance due on cash loans, both secured and unsecured. Contact the office where you received the loan if you don't have these figures. $_____

TAXES Federal and state income taxes or property taxes due now (including any that are past due). Don't list property taxes if they are automatically included in your mortgage payment. Check your income or property tax statements. If you're self-employed, you should include any Social Security taxes due. $_____

REAL ESTATE LOANS Balance you owe on deeds of trust (mortgages) on your property. Contact the office where you received the loan if you don't have these figures. Also list any liens on property that you are liable for and must pay. $_____

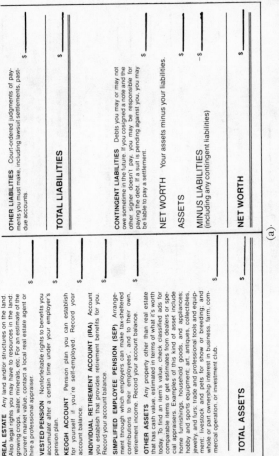

(a).

Figure 1.3 Personal financial statements: (a) Balance Sheet; (b) Income and Expense Statement. (Reprinted with permission from Bank of America, NT & SA, "How to Prepare a Personal Financial Statement," The Circular Series of Consumer Information Reports, copyright 1986.)[Part (b) follows.]

Income and Expense Statement

From _____ 19 ___ to _____, 19 ___

INCOME Money you receive.

GROSS SALARY, WAGES $ _____

MINUS DEDUCTIONS Federal and
state income tax, FICA, Social Security,
health insurance, etc.   – $ _____

TAKE-HOME PAY $ _____

**OTHER GROSS SALARY, WAGES
IN HOUSEHOLD** $ _____

MINUS DEDUCTIONS   – $ _____

TAKE-HOME PAY $ _____

COMMISSIONS, TIPS, BONUSES $ _____

**NET PROFIT FROM BUSINESS, FARM, TRADE,
PROFESSION** $ _____

**INTEREST OR DIVIDENDS FROM SAVINGS,
STOCKS, BONDS, OTHER SECURITIES, NOTES** $ _____

NET PROFIT FROM SALE OF ASSETS $ _____

NET PROFIT FROM RENTAL PROPERTY $ _____

PAYMENTS FROM OTHERS Alimony, child support. $ _____

REFUNDS, REBATES $ _____

CASH GIFTS $ _____

EXPENSES Money you spend, including self-established saving goals.

RENT Include utility payments if automatically included in rent. $ _____

MORTGAGE PAYMENTS Include property tax and insurance if automatically included in payment. $ _____

OTHER REAL ESTATE Second mortgage, home improvement loan (if secured by home), vacation home, storage rental, homeowners association fees. $ _____

HOUSEHOLD MAINTENANCE, REPAIR Gardening, housecleaning, appliance repairs (material, labor). $ _____

UTILITIES Gas, electricity, heating, fuel, phone, water, cable TV, garbage. $ _____

FOOD Groceries, nonfood items in supermarket bill. $ _____

TRANSPORTATION Car operating expenses (gas, oil, repairs, servicing), parking, public transportation. $ _____

CREDIT, CHARGE ACCOUNTS Payments for charge accounts, credit cards, personal lines of credit. $ _____

INSTALLMENT CONTRACT PAYMENTS Payments made at regular intervals over specific time periods for purchase of vehicle, mobile home, furniture, etc. $ _____

INSURANCE Real property (fire, liability, theft, etc., if not included in mortgage payment), personal property (homeowners, renters, auto), life, health, other. $ _____

INCOME TAXES Federal and state taxes due in addition to taxes withheld. $ _____

SOCIAL SECURITY BENEFITS	$ ___
IRAS, SEPS, KEOGHS	$ ___
PENSIONS, ANNUITIES	$ ___
VETERANS BENEFITS	$ ___
UNEMPLOYMENT BENEFITS	$ ___
DISABILITY BENEFITS	$ ___
LIFE INSURANCE BENEFITS	$ ___
INCOME FROM TRUSTS	$ ___
ROYALTIES, RESIDUALS	$ ___
OTHER INCOME	$ ___
TOTAL INCOME	**$ ___**
TOTAL INCOME	$ ___
MINUS TOTAL EXPENSES	– $ ___
DISCRETIONARY INCOME	**$ ___**

PROPERTY TAXES If not part of mortgage payment.	$ ___
OTHER TAXES Gift or estate taxes, for example.	$ ___
PAYMENTS TO OTHERS Alimony, child support.	$ ___
PERSONAL MAINTENANCE Clothing, laundry, barber, beauty salon, health and beauty products.	$ ___
SELF-IMPROVEMENT, EDUCATION Books, magazines, newspapers, seminars, lessons, tuition, room and board away from home.	$ ___
RECREATION, ENTERTAINMENT Restaurants, movies, sports, vacations, weekends, parties.	$ ___
SAVINGS Savings accounts, Christmas Clubs, time deposits, U.S. Savings Bonds, and so on.	$ ___
PERSONAL PROPERTY LEASE PAYMENTS Auto, furniture, equipment.	$ ___
REGULAR CONTRIBUTIONS Church, charities, other.	$ ___
DUES Union, club, and other memberships.	$ ___
CHILD CARE Day care, nursery school, housekeeper, babysitter.	$ ___
MEDICAL, DENTAL Drugs and treatments not covered by insurance. Also include transportation costs.	$ ___
TOTAL EXPENSES	$ ___

(b)

Figure 1.3 continued.

- It allows planning for situations when increases in income are not going to keep up with increased expenses.
- It shows where expenses can be selectively reduced.
- It enables the paying of bills on time.
- It assures that spending (e.g., credit cards) is within predetermined limits.
- It enables setting timetables for major purchases (e.g., buying a house).

Factors to be considered in determining the budget include your age, children's ages, hobbies, liquidity, health, and tax status.

There are differences involved in deriving monthly budget estimates. Income does not always come in evenly each month. Bonuses are given at year-end. Dividends are received quarterly. It is most difficult to estimate expenses for personal maintenance, such as food, clothing, and medicine. The amount may vary from month to month. **Tip:** Actual expenses should be compared to estimated expenses each month.

Recommendation: Be conservative in preparing a cash inflow forecast, since it is better to underestimate. If you overestimate cash inflows, you may be planning for and incurring expenses you cannot meet.

When planning your expenses, you will know some of them by heart (e.g., monthly loan payment, rent). Other expense predictions will require reference to your checkbook, credit card statements, and purchase receipts when cash has been paid.

In preparing an annual budget, you should show budgeted figures for each of the 12 months and a total column. An illustrative budget is shown in Figure 1.4.

A "Money Planner Worksheet" prepared by Bank of New York compares actual to goal figures for revenues and expenses (see Figure 1.5).

Looking at the worksheet, you should note several items. The

BEGINNING CASH BALANCE		$15,000
CASH RECEIPTS		
Salary—Husband	$40,000	
Salary—Wife	20,000	
Interest income	5,000	
Dividend income	2,000	
Royalty income	3,000	
Gifts	6,000	
Tax refunds	4,000	
Sale of securities	7,000	
Sale of assets	5,000	
Total cash receipts		$92,000
CASH EXPENSES		
Rent	$ 4,000	
Mortgage	3,000	
Fuel bills	1,000	
Telephone	2,000	
Electricity	600	
Gas expense	400	
Water	1,000	
Loan payments	4,000	
Education expense	3,000	
Property taxes	4,000	
Income taxes	2,000	
Insurance payments	6,000	
Medical bills	8,000	
Food	10,000	
Household items	12,000	
Furniture	14,000	
Clothing	6,000	
Transportation costs	5,000	
Entertainment expense	2,000	
Gift payments	1,000	
Personal care	1,000	
Total cash payments		90,000
Increase in cash flow		2,000
Ending cash balance		$17,000

Figure 1.4 Sample cash budget.

Money Planner Worksheet

NET INCOME

SOURCES These could include wages, alimony, child support, pensions, and so on. For more categories, see *How to Prepare a Personal Financial Statement*, another report in this series.

	Annual	Monthly
	————	————
	————	————
	————	————
TOTAL INCOME	$ ————	$ ————

EXPENSES

	Annual		Monthly	
	Now	Goal	Now	Goal

HOUSING

Rent, home loan payment				
Property taxes, assessments*				
Property insurance (homeowner, tenant)*				
Maintenance, repairs				
Utilities				
Gas, electricity				
Other fuel				
Telephone				
Water, sewer				
Cable TV				
Garbage collection				
Home furnishings*				
Other (such as homeowners association fees, household help other than child care)				

PERSONAL MAINTENANCE

Food				
Clothing				
Purchases				
Laundry, drycleaning, repairs				

Figure 1.5 Money planner worksheet. (Source: *Personal Money Planner*, Bank of New York, Circular Information Report, 1986.)

	Annual		Monthly	
	Now	Goal	Now	Goal

PERSONAL MAINTENANCE (cont'd.)

Self-Improvement

  Education

  Books, magazines, newspapers

Entertainment, recreation

  Vacations*

  Other (including movies, sports, restaurants, hobbies)

Transportation

  Gas, oil

  Repairs, maintenance*

  Parking, tolls

  Auto insurance

  License registration

  Public transportation

  Cabfare

Gifts, holiday expenses (other than Christmas Club accounts)

Child/dependent care (including babysitters, nursery school fees, convalescent care)

Health care

  Health insurance

  Doctors' visits

  Prescriptions, medicine

Personal care (including barber, hairdresser, cosmetics)*

OBLIGATIONS

Regular payments to others (including alimony, child support, other court-ordered payments)

Contributions, dues (voluntary, including those deducted from your paycheck)

(cont'd.)

	Annual		Monthly	
	Now	Goal	Now	Goal
OBLIGATIONS (cont'd.)				
Debt payments				
Installment loan payments (for vehicles, furniture, etc.)	___	___	___	___
Credit card, charge accounts	___	___	___	___
SAVINGS AND INVESTMENTS				
Short-term savings (including Christmas Club, emergency fund)	___	___	___	___
Long-term savings (including company or private pension, certificates of deposit)	___	___	___	___
Life insurance	___	___	___	___
Investments (including stocks, bonds, real estate)	___	___	___	___
TOTAL EXPENSE	$___	$___	$___	$___

*Set-aside account

Figure 1.5   continued.

goal may be either to limit spending or to increase it in certain areas. Is the goal realistic? Organize bills so that you know how much you owe and to whom. Is payment current or past due?

Recommendation: To take inflation into account, expense projections should incorporate the expected inflation rate. For example, if clothing is currently $1000 and inflation is forecasted at 5 percent, the budgeted figure is $1050.

EXAMPLE 1.4

Your beginning cash balance on 1/1/19X8 is $50,000. Taxable sources of income (e.g., salaries, interest, dividends) are $60,000.

Nontax sources of income (e.g., gifts) are $25,000. Tax-deductible expenses (e.g., interest on mortgage, property taxes) are $30,000. Nondeductible expenses (e.g., entertainment, clothing) are $15,000. Your tax rate is 28 percent. The ending cash balance on 12/31/19X8 is:

Cash balance—1/1/19X8		$50,000
Cash receipts:		
Taxable receipts ($60,000 × .72)	43,200	
Nontaxable receipts	25,000	68,200
		$118,200
Cash payments:		
Taxable payments ($30,000 × .72)	21,600	
Nontaxable payments	15,000	36,600
Cash balance—12/31/19X8		$81,600

What about Your Savings?

To be conservative and safe, you should have at least six months' income in a savings account. However, three to six months is more realistic for most people. **Recommendation:** Try to put 10 percent of gross income each period into savings. If you tie up your last cent in stocks and bonds, you may have to sell them when they are down in price. You need to have a basic amount of money saved for ordinary living expenses and emergencies.

Have more in a savings account if your income fluctuates sharply. Also have a backup fund that can be tapped if needed. The backup fund should be about the same amount as that in your liquid bank account. A backup fund may be in the form of a certificate of deposit.

Take full advantage of a pension plan, since your contributions and interest earned on them are tax-deferred. You are also accumulating a nest egg for old age.

Conclusion

Personal financial statements can be prepared showing how much you are worth. They enable you to properly manage assets and liabilities in terms of return and risk. For example, monitoring debt status is important, to assure you do not owe more than you can pay. The preparation of a budget facilitates the meeting of goals and the planning of income and expenses for the upcoming months.

2

Basic Time Value Applications

In making your financial decisions, such as annual loan payments or investment accumulation, you may need to use future value and present value tables that take into account the time value of money. You may want to know how much you have to invest each year to have a desired balance at retirement. You may desire to calculate the interest rate you are being charged on an auto loan. You may have to figure out how many years it will be before you can buy a house. These are just a few of the many practical applications that the tables offer.

Using Future Value Tables in Decision Making

Future (compound) value of money is important to consider in making investment decisions. You can solve for different unknowns, such as accumulated amount, annual payment, interest rate, and number of periods. Here are some guidelines for using future value tables.

- A future value table is used if you want to determine the future (later) amount of cash flows paid or received.

- The "Future Value of $1" table is used if you have unequal cash flows each period or a lump-sum cash flow.

- The "Future Value of Annuity of $1" table is used if the cash flows each period are equal and occur at the end of the period.

- If you want to determine a total dollar amount in the future, you have a multiplication problem.

- If you want to calculate an annual payment, interest rate, or number of periods, you have a division problem. In such a case, what you put in the numerator of a fraction determines which table to use. For example, if you put in the numerator a future value that involves equal year-end payments, you have to use a "Future Value of Annuity of $1" Table.

- If you are solving for an annual payment, divide the numerator by the factor corresponding to the interest rate (i) and the number of periods (n).

- If you are solving for an interest rate, divide the numerator by the annual payment to get a factor. Then, to find the interest rate, find the factor on the table opposite the number of years. The interest rate will be indicated at the top of the column where the factor is located.

- If you are solving for the number of years, divide the numerator by the annual payment to get the factor. Then find the factor in the appropriate interest rate column. The number of years will be indicated in the far left-hand column.

Now let us look at situations in which you may actually solve problems using the future value tables.

The "Future Value of $1" Table

This computation indicates the increased value of a single sum of money over a certain future time period. A determination must be made of what money will be worth tomorrow (see Table 2.1).

EXAMPLE 2.1

You deposit $5000 in a mutual fund that will earn a 10 percent annual return. You will invest the money for six years. The accumulated amount is:

$$\$5\,000 \times 1.77156 = \$8858$$

EXAMPLE 2.2

You put $400 in a savings account earning 10 percent interest compounded annually for six years. You will have accumulated:

$$\$400 \times 1.77156 = \$709$$

EXAMPLE 2.3

Your current salary is $30,000. You anticipate receiving a 4 percent pay raise each year. Your salary in 10 years will be:

$$\$30,000 \times 1.48024 = \$44,407.$$

EXAMPLE 2.4

You bought a house today for $150,000 that you plan to sell in 15 years. The expected annual growth rate is 12 percent. The anticipated value of the house at the end of the fifteenth year is:

$$\$150,000 \times 5.47357 = \$821,036$$

Table 2.1 Future Value of $1*

$$a_{\overline{n}|i} = (1 + i)^n$$

(n) Periods	2%	2½%	3%	4%	5%	6%
1	1.02000	1.02500	1.03000	1.04000	1.05000	1.06000
2	1.04040	1.05063	1.06090	1.08160	1.10250	1.12360
3	1.06121	1.07689	1.09273	1.12486	1.15763	1.19102
4	1.08243	1.10381	1.12551	1.16986	1.21551	1.26248
5	1.10408	1.13141	1.15927	1.21665	1.27628	1.33823
6	1.12616	1.15969	1.19405	1.26532	1.34010	1.41852
7	1.14869	1.18869	1.22987	1.31593	1.40710	1.50363
8	1.17166	1.21840	1.26677	1.36857	1.47746	1.59385
9	1.19509	1.24886	1.30477	1.42331	1.55133	1.68948
10	1.21899	1.28008	1.34392	1.48024	1.62889	1.79085
11	1.24337	1.31209	1.38423	1.53945	1.71034	1.89830
12	1.26824	1.34489	1.42576	1.60103	1.79586	2.01220
13	1.29361	1.37851	1.46853	1.66507	1.88565	2.13293
14	1.31948	1.41297	1.51259	1.73168	1.97993	2.26090
15	1.34587	1.44830	1.55797	1.80094	2.07893	2.39656
16	1.37279	1.48451	1.60471	1.87298	2.18287	2.54035
17	1.40024	1.52162	1.65285	1.94790	2.29202	2.69277
18	1.42825	1.55966	1.70243	2.02582	2.40662	2.85434
19	1.45681	1.59865	1.75351	2.10685	2.52695	3.02560
20	1.48595	1.63862	1.80611	2.19112	2.65330	3.20714
21	1.51567	1.67958	1.86029	2.27877	2.78596	3.39956
22	1.54598	1.72157	1.91610	2.36992	2.92526	3.60354
23	1.57690	1.76461	1.97359	2.46472	3.07152	3.81975
24	1.60844	1.80873	2.03279	2.56330	3.22510	4.04893
25	1.64061	1.85394	2.09378	2.66584	3.38635	4.29187
26	1.67342	1.90029	2.15659	2.77247	3.55567	4.54938
27	1.70689	1.94780	2.22129	2.88337	3.73346	4.82235
28	1.74102	1.99650	2.28793	2.99870	3.92013	5.11169
29	1.77584	2.04641	2.35657	3.11865	4.11614	5.41839
30	1.81136	2.09757	2.42726	3.24340	4.32194	5.74349
31	1.84759	2.15001	2.50008	3.37313	4.53804	6.08810
32	1.88454	2.20376	2.57508	3.50806	4.76494	6.45339
33	1.92223	2.25885	2.65234	3.64838	5.00319	6.84059
34	1.96068	2.31532	2.73191	3.79432	5.25335	7.25103
35	1.99989	2.37321	2.81386	3.94609	5.51602	7.68609
36	2.03989	2.43254	2.89828	4.10393	5.79182	8.14725
37	2.08069	2.49335	2.98523	4.26809	6.08141	8.63609
38	2.12230	2.55568	3.07478	4.43881	6.38548	9.15425
39	2.16474	2.61957	3.16703	4.61637	6.70475	9.70351
40	2.20804	2.68506	3.26204	4.80102	7.03999	10.28572

*Tables are reprinted with permission from Kieso and Weygandt, *Intermediate Accounting* (New York: John Wiley, 1983).

8%	9%	10%	11%	12%	15%	(n) Periods
1.08000	1.09000	1.10000	1.11000	1.12000	1.15000	1
1.16640	1.18810	1.21000	1.23210	1.25440	1.32250	2
1.25971	1.29503	1.33100	1.36763	1.40493	1.52088	3
1.36049	1.41158	1.46410	1.51807	1.57352	1.74901	4
1.46933	1.53862	1.61051	1.68506	1.76234	2.01136	5
1.58687	1.67710	1.77156	1.87041	1.97382	2.31306	6
1.71382	1.82804	1.94872	2.07616	2.21068	2.66002	7
1.85093	1.99256	2.14359	2.30454	2.47596	3.05902	8
1.99900	2.17189	2.35795	2.55803	2.77308	3.51788	9
2.15892	2.36736	2.59374	2.83942	3.10585	4.04556	10
2.33164	2.58043	2.85312	3.15176	3.47855	4.65239	11
2.51817	2.81267	3.13843	3.49845	3.89598	5.35025	12
2.71962	3.06581	3.45227	3.88328	4.36349	6.15279	13
2.93719	3.34173	3.79750	4.31044	4.88711	7.07571	14
3.17217	3.64248	4.17725	4.78459	5.47357	8.13706	15
3.42594	3.97031	4.59497	5.31089	6.13039	9.35762	16
3.70002	4.32763	5.05447	5.89509	6.86604	10.76126	17
3.99602	4.71712	5.55992	6.54355	7.68997	12.37545	18
4.31570	5.14166	6.11591	7.26334	8.61276	14.23177	19
4.66096	5.60441	6.72750	8.06231	9.64629	16.36654	20
5.03383	6.10881	7.40025	8.94917	10.80385	18.82152	21
5.43654	6.65860	8.14028	9.93357	12.10031	21.64475	22
5.87146	7.25787	8.95430	11.02627	13.55235	24.89146	23
6.34118	7.91108	9.84973	12.23916	15.17863	28.62518	24
6.84847	8.62308	10.83471	13.58546	17.00000	32.91895	25
7.39635	9.39916	11.91818	15.07986	19.04007	37.85680	26
7.98806	10.24508	13.10999	16.73865	21.32488	43.53532	27
8.62711	11.16714	14.42099	18.57990	23.88387	50.06561	28
9.31727	12.17218	15.86309	20.62369	26.74993	57.57545	29
10.06266	13.26768	17.44940	22.89230	29.95992	66.21177	30
10.86767	14.46177	19.19434	25.41045	33.55511	76.14354	31
11.73708	15.76333	21.11378	28.20560	37.58173	87.56507	32
12.67605	17.18203	23.22515	31.30821	42.09153	100.69983	33
13.69013	18.72841	25.54767	34.75212	47.14252	115.80480	34
14.78534	20.41397	28.10244	38.57485	52.79962	133.17552	35
15.96817	22.25123	30.91268	42.81808	59.13557	153.15185	36
17.24563	24.25384	34.00395	47.52807	66.23144	176.12465	37
18.62528	26.43668	37.40434	52.75616	74.17966	202.54332	38
20.11530	28.81598	41.14479	58.55934	83.08122	232.92482	39
21.72452	31.40942	45.25926	65.00087	93.05097	267.86355	40

EXAMPLE 2.5

You deposit $10,000 in an account offering an annual interest rate of 20 percent. You will keep the money on deposit for five years. The interest is compounded quarterly. The accumulated amount at the end of the fifth year is:

$$n = 5 \times 4 = 20$$
$$i = 20\%/4 = 5\%$$
$$\$10,000 \times 2.65330 = \$26,533$$

EXAMPLE 2.6

You invest $10,000 today in a bank account. It is to be kept in the bank for five years at 12 percent. The accumulated amount equals:

$$\$10,000 \times 1.76234 = \$17,623$$

If interest is compounded quarterly, the accumulated amount equals:

$$n = 5 \times 4 = 20$$
$$i = 12\%/4 = 3\%$$
$$\$10,000 \times 1.80611 = \$18,061$$

The reason that the accumulated amount with quarterly compounding is more than annual compounding is that greater compounding of interest exists.

EXAMPLE 2.7

You want to have $1,000,000 at the end of 15 years. The interest rate is 8 percent. You have to deposit today the following sum to accomplish your objective:

$$\frac{\$1,000,000}{3.17217} = \$315,242$$

EXAMPLE 2.8

At an interest rate of 12 percent, you want to know how long it will take for your money to double.

$$\frac{\$2}{\$1} = 2$$

n = 6 years (approximate)

EXAMPLE 2.9

You want to have $250,000. Your initial deposit is $30,000. The interest rate is 12 percent. The number of years it will take to reach your goal is:

$$\frac{\$250,000}{\$30,000} = 8.3333$$

n = 18.5 years (approximate)

The factor falls about midway between 18 and 19 years.

EXAMPLE 2.10

You agree to pay back $3000 in six years on a $2000 loan made today. You are being charged an interest rate of:

$$\frac{\$3000}{\$2000} = 1.5$$

i = 7%

EXAMPLE 2.11

Your salary was $12,000 in 19X1 and eight years later it is $36,700. The compound annual growth rate is:

$$\frac{\$36,700}{\$12,000} = 3.05833$$

Growth rate = 15% (approximate)

The "Future Value of Annuity of $1" Table

You can also compute the increased value of equal payments over time (Table 2.2).

EXAMPLE 2.12

You plan to put $20,000 in a savings account at the end of each year for the next 15 years. The interest rate is 8 percent. The accumulated balance at the end of the 15th year is:

$20,000 × 27.15211 = $543,042.

EXAMPLE 2.13

You deposit $1000 per month for two years. The interest rate is 24 percent. Your accumulated balance is:

$n = 2 \times 12 = 24$
$i = 24\%/12 = 2\%$
$1000 × 30.42186 = $30,422

EXAMPLE 2.14

You want to determine the annual year-end deposit needed to accumulate $100,000 at the end of 15 years. The interest rate is 12 percent. The annual deposit is:

$$\frac{\$100,000}{37.27972} = \$2,682$$

EXAMPLE 2.15

You want to have $500,000 accumulated in your mutual fund. You make four deposits of $100,000 per year. The interest rate you must earn is:

$$\frac{\$500,000}{\$100,000} = 5$$

$$i = 15\% \text{ (approximate)}$$

EXAMPLE 2.16

You want $500,000 in the future. The interest rate is 10 percent. The annual payment is $80,000. The number of years it will take to accomplish this objective is:

$$\frac{\$500,000}{\$80,000} = 6.25$$

$$n = 5 \text{ years (approximate)}$$

Using Present Value Tables in Decision Making

Present (discount) value of money is considered in personal financial planning decisions. Different unknowns may be solved for, such as present value amount, annual payment, interest rate, and number of periods. Guidelines for using the tables follow:

- A present value table is used if you want to determine the *current* amount of receiving or paying future cash flows.
- The "Present Value of $1" table (Table 2.3) is used if you have unequal cash flows each period or a lump-sum cash flow.
- The "Present Value of Annuity of $1" table (Table 2.4) is used if the cash flows each period are equal.

The "Present Value of $1" Table

Present value is the opposite of compounding. By knowing what something is worth in a later year, you can find out its value today.

Table 2.2 Future Value of an Annuity of $1

$$A_{\overline{n}|} = \frac{(1 + i)^n - 1}{i}$$

(n) Periods	2%	2½%	3%	4%	5%	6%
1	1.00000	1.00000	1.00000	1.00000	1.00000	1.00000
2	2.02000	2.02500	2.03000	2.04000	2.05000	2.06000
3	3.06040	3.07563	3.09090	3.12160	3.15250	3.18360
4	4.12161	4.15252	4.18363	4.24646	4.31013	4.37462
5	5.20404	5.25633	5.30914	5.41632	5.52563	5.63709
6	6.30812	6.38774	6.46841	6.63298	6.80191	6.97532
7	7.43428	7.54743	7.66246	7.89829	8.14201	8.39384
8	8.58297	8.73612	8.89234	9.21423	9.54911	9.89747
9	9.75463	9.95452	10.15911	10.58280	11.02656	11.49132
10	10.94972	11.20338	11.46338	12.00611	12.57789	13.18079
11	12.16872	12.48347	12.80780	13.48635	14.20679	14.97164
12	13.41209	13.79555	14.19203	15.02581	15.91713	16.86994
13	14.68033	15.14044	15.61779	16.62684	17.71298	18.88214
14	15.97394	16.51895	17.08632	18.29191	19.59863	21.01507
15	17.29342	17.93193	18.59891	20.02359	21.57856	23.27597
16	18.63929	19.38022	20.15688	21.82453	23.65749	25.67253
17	20.01207	20.86473	21.76159	23.69751	25.84037	28.21288
18	21.41231	22.38635	23.41444	25.64541	28.13238	30.90565
19	22.84056	23.94601	25.11687	27.67123	30.53900	33.75999
20	24.29737	25.54466	26.87037	29.77808	33.06595	36.78559
21	25.78332	27.18327	28.67649	31.96920	35.71925	39.99273
22	27.29898	28.86286	30.53678	34.24797	38.50521	43.39229
23	28.84496	30.58443	32.45288	36.61789	41.43048	46.99583
24	30.42186	32.34904	34.42647	39.08260	44.50200	50.81558
25	32.03030	34.15776	36.45926	41.64591	47.72710	54.86451
26	33.67091	36.01171	38.55304	44.31174	51.11345	59.15638
27	35.34432	37.91200	40.70963	47.08421	54.66913	63.70577
28	37.05121	39.85980	42.93092	49.96758	58.40258	68.52811
29	38.79223	41.85630	45.21885	52.96629	62.32271	73.63980
30	40.56808	43.90270	47.57542	56.08494	66.43885	79.05819
31	42.37944	46.00027	50.00268	59.32834	70.76079	84.80168
32	44.22703	48.15028	52.50276	62.70147	75.29883	90.88978
33	46.11157	50.35403	55.07784	66.20953	80.06377	97.34316
34	48.03380	52.61289	57.73018	69.85791	85.06696	104.18376
35	49.99448	54.92821	60.46208	73.65222	90.32031	111.43478
36	51.99437	57.30141	63.27594	77.59831	95.83632	119.12087
37	54.03425	59.73395	66.17422	81.70225	101.62814	127.26812
38	56.11494	62.22730	69.15945	85.97034	107.70955	135.90421
39	58.23724	64.78298	72.23423	90.40915	114.09502	145.05846
40	60.40198	67.40255	75.40126	95.02552	120.79977	154.76197

8%	9%	10%	11%	12%	15%	(n) Periods
1.00000	1.00000	1.00000	1.00000	1.00000	1.00000	1
2.08000	2.09000	2.10000	2.11000	2.12000	2.15000	2
3.24640	3.27810	3.31000	3.34210	3.37440	3.47250	3
4.50611	4.57313	4.64100	4.70973	4.77933	4.99338	4
5.86660	5.98471	6.10510	6.22780	6.35285	6.74238	5
7.33592	7.52334	7.71561	7.91286	8.11519	8.75374	6
8.92280	9.20044	9.48717	9.78327	10.08901	11.06680	7
10.63663	11.02847	11.43589	11.85943	12.29969	13.72682	8
12.48756	13.02104	13.57948	14.16397	14.77566	16.78584	9
14.48656	15.19293	15.93743	16.72201	17.54874	20.30372	10
16.64549	17.56029	18.53117	19.56143	20.65458	24.34928	11
18.97713	20.14072	21.38428	22.71319	24.13313	29.00167	12
21.49530	22.95339	24.52271	26.21164	28.02911	34.35192	13
24.21492	26.01919	27.97498	30.09492	32.39260	40.50471	14
27.15211	29.36092	31.77248	34.40536	37.27972	47.58041	15
30.32428	33.00340	35.94973	39.18995	42.75328	55.71747	16
33.75023	36.97371	40.54470	44.50084	48.88367	65.07509	17
37.45024	41.30134	45.59917	50.39593	55.74972	75.83636	18
41.44626	46.01846	51.15909	56.93949	63.43968	88.21181	19
45.76196	51.16012	57.27500	64.20283	72.05244	102.44358	20
50.42292	56.76453	64.00250	72.26514	81.69874	118.81012	21
55.45676	62.87334	71.40275	81.21431	92.50258	137.63164	22
60.89330	69.53194	79.54302	91.14788	104.60289	159.27638	23
66.76476	76.78981	88.49733	102.17415	118.15524	184.16784	24
73.10594	84.70090	98.34706	114.41331	133.33387	212.79302	25
79.95442	93.32398	109.18177	127.99877	150.33393	245.71197	26
87.35077	102.72314	121.09994	143.07864	169.37401	283.56877	27
95.33883	112.96822	134.20994	159.81729	190.69889	327.10408	28
103.96594	124.13536	148.63093	178.39719	214.58275	377.16969	29
113.28321	136.30754	164.49402	199.02088	241.33268	434.74515	30
123.34587	149.57522	181.94343	221.91317	271.29261	500.95692	31
134.21354	164.03699	201.13777	247.32362	304.84772	577.10046	32
145.95062	179.80032	222.25154	275.52922	342.42945	644.66553	33
158.62667	196.98234	245.47670	306.83744	384.52098	765.36535	34
172.31680	215.71076	271.02437	341.58955	431.66350	881.17016	35
187.10215	238.12472	299.12681	380.16441	484.46312	1014.34568	36
203.07032	258.37595	330.03949	422.98249	543.59869	1167.49753	37
220.31595	282.62978	364.04343	470.51056	609.83053	1343.62216	38
238.94122	309.06646	401.44778	523.26673	684.01020	1546.16549	39
259.05652	337.88245	442.59256	581.82607	767.09142	1779.09031	40

Table 2.3 Present Value of $1

$$p_{\overline{n}|} = \frac{1}{(1 + i)^n} = (1 + i)^{-n}$$

(n) Periods	2%	2½%	3%	4%	5%	6%
1	.98039	.97561	.97087	.96154	.95238	.94340
2	.96117	.95181	.94260	.92456	.90703	.89000
3	.94232	.92860	.91514	.88900	.86384	.83962
4	.92385	.90595	.88849	.85480	.82270	.79209
5	.90573	.88385	.86261	.82193	.78353	.74726
6	.88797	.86230	.83748	.79031	.74622	.70496
7	.87056	.84127	.81309	.75992	.71068	.66506
8	.85349	.82075	.78941	.73069	.67684	.62741
9	.83676	.80073	.76642	.70259	.64461	.59190
10	.82035	.78120	.74409	.67556	.61391	.55839
11	.80426	.76214	.72242	.64958	.58468	.52679
12	.78849	.74356	.70138	.62460	.55684	.49697
13	.77303	.72542	.68095	.60057	.53032	.46884
14	.75788	.70773	.66112	.57748	.50507	.44230
15	.74301	.69047	.64186	.55526	.48102	.41727
16	.72845	.67362	.62317	.53391	.45811	.39365
17	.71416	.65720	.60502	.51337	.43630	.37136
18	.70016	.64117	.58739	.49363	.41552	.35034
19	.68643	.62553	.57029	.47464	.39573	.33051
20	.67297	.61027	.55368	.45639	.37689	.31180
21	.65978	.59539	.53755	.43883	.35894	.29416
22	.64684	.58086	.52189	.42196	.34185	.27751
23	.63416	.56670	.50669	.40573	.32557	.26180
24	.62172	.55288	.49193	.39012	.31007	.24698
25	.60953	.53939	.47761	.37512	.29530	.23300
26	.59758	.52623	.46369	.36069	.28124	.21981
27	.58586	.51340	.45019	.34682	.26785	.20737
28	.57437	.50088	.43708	.33348	.25509	.19563
29	.56311	.48866	.42435	.32065	.24295	.18456
30	.55207	.47674	.41199	.30832	.23138	.17411
31	.54125	.46511	.39999	.29646	.22036	.16425
32	.53063	.45377	.38834	.28506	.20987	.15496
33	.52023	.44270	.37703	.27409	.19987	.14619
34	.51003	.43191	.36604	.26355	.19035	.13791
35	.50003	.42137	.35538	.25342	.18129	.13011
36	.49022	.41109	.34503	.24367	.17266	.12274
37	.48061	.40107	.33498	.23430	.16444	.11579
38	.47119	.39128	.32523	.22529	.15661	.10924
39	.46195	.38174	.31575	.21662	.14915	.10306
40	.45289	.37243	.30656	.20829	.14205	.09722

8%	9%	10%	11%	12%	15%	(n) Periods
.92593	.91743	.90909	.90090	.89286	.86957	1
.85734	.84168	.82645	.81162	.79719	.75614	2
.79383	.77218	.75132	.73119	.71178	.65752	3
.73503	.70843	.68301	.65873	.63552	.57175	4
.68058	.64993	.62092	.59345	.56743	.49718	5
.63017	.59627	.56447	.53464	.50663	.43233	6
.58349	.54703	.51316	.48166	.45235	.37594	7
.54027	.50187	.46651	.43393	.40388	.32690	8
.50025	.46043	.42410	.39092	.36061	.28426	9
.46319	.42241	.38554	.35218	.32197	.24719	10
.42888	.38753	.35049	.31728	.28748	.21494	11
.39711	.35554	.31863	.28584	.25668	.18691	12
.36770	.32618	.28966	.25751	.22917	.16253	13
.34046	.29925	.26333	.23199	.20462	.14133	14
.31524	.27454	.23939	.20900	.18270	.12289	15
.29189	.25187	.21763	.18829	.16312	.10687	16
.27027	.23107	.19785	.16963	.14564	.09293	17
.25025	.21199	.17986	.15282	.13004	.08081	18
.23171	.19449	.16351	.13768	.11611	.07027	19
.21455	.17843	.14864	.12403	.10367	.06110	20
.19866	.16370	.13513	.11174	.09256	.05313	21
.18394	.15018	.12285	.10067	.08264	.04620	22
.17032	.13778	.11168	.09069	.07379	.04017	23
.15770	.12641	.10153	.08170	.06588	.03493	24
.14602	.11597	.09230	.07361	.05882	.03038	25
.13520	.10639	.08391	.06631	.05252	.02642	26
.12519	.09761	.07628	.05974	.04689	.02297	27
.11591	.08955	.06934	.05382	.04187	.01997	28
.10733	.08216	.06304	.04849	.03738	.01737	29
.09938	.07537	.05731	.04368	.03338	.01510	30
.09202	.06915	.05210	.03935	.02980	.01313	31
.08520	.06344	.04736	.03545	.02661	.01142	32
.07889	.05820	.04306	.03194	.02376	.00993	33
.07305	.05340	.03914	.02878	.02121	.00864	34
.06763	.04899	.03558	.02592	.01894	.00751	35
.06262	.04494	.03235	.02335	.01691	.00653	36
.05799	.04123	.02941	.02104	.01510	.00568	37
.05369	.03783	.02674	.01896	.01348	.00494	38
.04971	.03470	.02430	.01708	.01204	.00429	39
.04603	.03184	.02210	.01538	.01075	.00373	40

Table 2.4 Present Value of an Annuity of $1

$$p_{\overline{n}|i} = \frac{1 - \dfrac{1}{(1 + i)^n}}{i} = \frac{1 - p_{\overline{n}|i}}{i}$$

(n) Periods	2%	2½%	3%	4%	5%	6%
1	.98039	.97561	.97087	.96154	.95238	.94340
2	1.94156	1.92742	1.91347	1.88609	1.85941	1.83339
3	2.88388	2.85602	2.82861	2.77509	2.72325	2.67301
4	3.80773	3.76197	3.71710	3.62990	3.54595	3.46511
5	4.71346	4.64583	4.57971	4.45182	4.32948	4.21236
6	5.60143	5.50813	5.41719	5.24214	5.07569	4.91732
7	6.47199	6.34939	6.23028	6.00205	5.78637	5.58238
8	7.32548	7.17014	7.01969	6.73274	6.46321	6.20979
9	8.16224	7.97087	7.78611	7.43533	7.10782	6.80169
10	8.98259	8.75206	8.53020	8.11090	7.72173	7.36009
11	9.78685	9.51421	9.25262	8.76048	8.30641	7.88687
12	10.57534	10.25776	9.95400	9.38507	8.86325	8.38384
13	11.34837	10.98319	10.63496	9.98565	9.39357	8.85268
14	12.10625	11.69091	11.29607	10.56312	9.89864	9.29498
15	12.84926	12.38138	11.93794	11.11839	10.37966	9.71225
16	13.57771	13.05500	12.56110	11.65230	10.83777	10.10590
17	14.29187	13.71220	13.16612	12.16567	11.27407	10.47726
18	14.99203	14.35336	13.75351	12.65930	11.68959	10.82760
19	15.67846	14.97889	14.32380	13.13394	12.08532	11.15812
20	16.35143	15.58916	14.87747	13.59033	12.46221	11.46992
21	17.01121	16.18455	15.41502	14.02916	12.82115	11.76408
22	17.65805	16.76541	15.93692	14.45112	13.16300	12.04158
23	18.29220	17.33211	16.44361	14.85684	13.48857	12.30338
24	18.91393	17.88499	16.93554	15.24696	13.79864	12.55036
25	19.52346	18.42438	17.41315	15.62208	14.09394	12.78336
26	20.12104	18.95061	17.87684	15.98277	14.37519	13.00317
27	20.70690	19.46401	18.32703	16.32959	14.64303	13.21053
28	21.28127	19.96489	18.76411	16.66306	14.89813	13.40616
29	21.84438	20.45355	19.18845	16.98371	15.14107	13.59072
30	22.39646	20.93029	19.60044	17.29203	15.37245	13.76483
31	22.93770	21.39541	20.00043	17.58849	15.59281	13.92909
32	23.46833	21.84918	20.38877	17.87355	15.80268	14.08404
33	23.98856	22.29188	20.76579	18.14765	16.00255	14.23023
34	24.49859	22.72379	21.13184	18.41120	16.19290	14.36814
35	24.99862	23.14516	21.48722	18.66461	16.37419	14.49825
36	25.48884	23.55625	21.83225	18.90828	16.54685	14.62099
37	25.96945	23.95732	22.16724	19.14258	16.71129	14.73678
38	26.44064	24.34860	22.49246	19.36786	16.86789	14.84602
39	26.90259	24.73034	22.80822	19.58448	17.01704	14.94907
40	27.35548	25.10278	23.11477	19.79277	17.15909	15.04630

8%	9%	10%	11%	12%	15%	(n) Periods
.92593	.91743	.90909	.90090	.89286	.86957	1
1.78326	1.75911	1.73554	1.71252	1.69005	1.62571	2
2.57710	2.53130	2.48685	2.44371	2.40183	2.28323	3
3.31213	3.23972	3.16986	3.10245	3.03735	2.85498	4
3.99271	3.88965	3.79079	3.69590	3.60478	3.35216	5
4.62288	4.48592	4.35526	4.23054	4.11141	3.78448	6
5.20637	5.03295	4.86842	4.71220	4.56376	4.16042	7
5.74664	5.53482	5.33493	5.14612	4.96764	4.48732	8
6.24689	5.99525	5.75902	5.53705	5.32825	4.77158	9
6.71008	6.41766	6.14457	5.88923	5.65022	5.01877	10
7.13896	6.80519	6.49506	6.20652	5.93770	5.23371	11
7.53608	7.16073	6.81369	6.49236	6.19437	5.42062	12
7.90378	7.48690	7.10336	6.74987	6.42355	5.58315	13
8.24424	7.78615	7.36669	6.98187	6.62817	5.72448	14
8.55948	8.06069	7.60608	7.19087	6.81086	5.84737	15
8.85137	8.31256	7.82371	7.37916	6.97399	5.95424	16
9.12164	8.54363	8.02155	7.54879	7.11963	6.04716	17
9.37189	8.75563	8.20141	7.70162	7.24967	6.12797	18
9.60360	8.95012	8.36492	7.83929	7.36578	6.19823	19
9.81815	9.12855	8.51356	7.96333	7.46944	6.25933	20
10.01680	9.29224	8.64869	8.07507	7.56200	6.31246	21
10.20074	9.44243	8.77154	8.17574	7.64465	6.35866	22
10.37106	9.58021	8.88322	8.26643	7.71843	6.39884	23
10.52876	9.70661	8.98474	8.34814	7.78432	6.43377	24
10.67478	9.82258	9.07704	8.42174	7.84314	6.46415	25
10.80998	9.92897	9.16095	8.48806	7.89566	6.49056	26
10.93516	10.02658	9.23722	8.54780	7.94255	6.51353	27
11.05108	10.11613	9.30657	8.60162	7.98442	6.53351	28
11.15841	10.19828	9.36961	8.65011	8.02181	6.55088	29
11.25778	10.27365	9.42691	8.69379	8.05518	6.56598	30
11.34980	10.34280	9.47901	8.73315	8.08499	6.57911	31
11.43500	10.40624	9.52638	8.76860	8.11159	6.59053	32
11.51389	10.46444	9.56943	8.80054	8.13535	6.60046	33
11.58693	10.51784	9.60858	8.82932	8.15656	6.60910	34
11.65457	10.56682	9.64416	8.85524	8.17550	6.61661	35
11.71719	10.61176	9.67651	8.87859	8.19241	6.62314	36
11.77518	10.65299	9.70592	8.89963	8.20751	6.62882	37
11.82887	10.69082	9.73265	8.91859	8.22099	6.63375	38
11.87858	10.72552	9.75697	8.93567	8.23303	6.63805	39
11.92461	10.75736	9.77905	8.95105	8.24378	6.64178	40

In effect, you are discounting a future amount to compute its current worth (See Table 2.3).

EXAMPLE 2.17

You have an opportunity to receive $30,000 four years from now. You earn 12 percent on your investment. The most you should pay for this investment is:

$30,000 × .63552 = $19,066

EXAMPLE 2.18

You will receive a $100,000 settlement from an insurance company at the end of seven years. The inflation rate is 9 percent. The present value of the settlement is:

$100,000 × .54703 = $54,703

EXAMPLE 2.19

You are 30 years old and plan to invest in a 25-year, zero-coupon bond yielding 10 percent. Upon retirement at age 60, you want to have accumulated $400,000. The investment needed today to accomplish this goal is:

$400,000 × .03558 = $14,232

EXAMPLE 2.20

You are thinking of investing $30,000. The interest rate is 10 percent. Your annual net cash inflows from the investment are:

Year 1	$ 8,000
Year 2	15,000
Year 3	18,000

The net present value of the investment is positive and the

investment should be made, as indicated in the following calculations:

Year	Calculation	Net present value
0	−$30,000 × 1	−$30,000
1	8,000 × .90909	7,273
2	15,000 × .82645	12,397
3	18,000 × .75132	13,524
Net present value		$3,194

The "Present Value of Annuity of $1" Table

This values a series of equal future payments, such as annuities received from pension plans and insurance policies, in today's dollars. When using this table, all you need to do is multiply the annual cash payment by the factor (Table 2.4).

EXAMPLE 2.21

You will receive $10,000 a year for six years at 10 percent. The present value is:

$10,000 × 4.35526 = $43,553

EXAMPLE 2.22

The terms of your divorce settlement are that you will receive monthly payments of $600 for three years. The discount rate is 24 percent. Today the settlement is worth:

$600 × 25.48884 = $15,293

EXAMPLE 2.23

You are trying to determine the price you are willing to pay for a $1000 five-year United States Savings Bond paying $50 interest semi-annually, which is sold to yield 8 percent. The present value is computed below.

$$i = 8\%/2 = 4\%$$
$$n = 5 \times 2 = 10$$

Present Value of $1 (Table 2.3) $1000 × .67556	$ 676
Present Value of an Annuity of $1 (Table 2.4) $50 − 8.11090	406
	$1082

EXAMPLE 2.24

You borrow $200,000 for five years at an interest rate of 12 percent. The annual year-end payment on the loan is:

$$\frac{\$200,000}{3.60478} = \$55,482$$

EXAMPLE 2.25

You take out a $30,000 loan payable monthly over three years. The annual interest rate is 24 percent. The monthly payment is:

$$\frac{\$30,000}{25.48884} = \$1177$$

EXAMPLE 2.26

You borrow $300,000, payable at $70,000 a year. The interest rate is 12 percent. The number of years you have to pay off the loan is:

$$\frac{\$300,000}{\$70,000} = 4.2857$$

$$n = 6 \text{ years (approximate)}$$

EXAMPLE 2.27

You borrow $20,000, to be repaid in 12 monthly payments of $1,891.20. The monthly interest rate is:

$$\frac{\$20,000.00}{\$1891.20} = 10.5753$$

$$i = 2\%$$

EXAMPLE 2.28

You borrow $1,000,000 and agree to make payments of $100,000 per year for 18 years. The interest rate you are paying is:

$$\frac{\$1,000,000}{\$100,000} = 10$$

$$i = 7\% \text{ (approximate)}$$

EXAMPLE 2.29

When you retire you want to receive an annuity of $80,000 at the end of each year for 10 years. The interest rate is 8 percent. The amount that must be in your retirement account at the date of retirement is computed below.

$$\$80,000 \times 6.71008 = \$536,806$$

EXAMPLE 2.30

You have $300,000 in your pension plan today. You want to take an annuity for 20 years at an interest rate of 12 percent. The amount you will receive each year is:

$$\frac{\$300,000}{7.46944} = \$40,164$$

EXAMPLE 2.31

If you buy a car, you have to give a 10 percent down payment on a list price of $10,000 and finance the balance over three years at an interest rate of 12 percent. The annual payment required on the lease agreement is:

$$\frac{\$9000}{2.40183} = \$3747$$

Conclusion

By using future value and present value tables, you can make many financial decisions that are in your best interest. You can solve for accumulated amount, present value amount, annual payment, interest rate, and number of periods.

3

What You Should Know about Investments and Planning

Financial Assets and Real Assets

The two basic kinds of investments are financial assets and real assets. *Financial assets* comprise all intangible assets: they might represent equity ownership of a company, or provide evidence that someone owes you a debt, or show your right to buy or sell your ownership interest at a later date. Financial assets include:

- Common stock
- Options and warrants
- Mutual funds
- Savings accounts, money market certificates, and money market funds
- Treasury bills
- Commercial paper
- Bonds
- Preferred stock

- Commodity futures
- Financial futures

Real assets are those investments you can put your hands on. They are what we call real property. Real assets include:

- Real estate
- Precious metals
- Collectibles and gems
- Common stocks
- Oil

What proportion of your assets are financial, what proportion real?

Investing: Short-Term and Long-Term

An investment may be short-term or long-term. Short-term investments are held for one year or less, whereas long-term investments mature after more than one year. An example of a short-term investment is a one-year certificate of deposit; a typical long-term investment is a ten-year bond. (Some long-term investments have no maturity date.) Equity securities (common stock and preferred stock) are considered long-term investments. But you can purchase a long-term investment and treat it as a short-term investment by selling it within one year. What is your mix of short-term and long-term investments?

Some Investment Considerations

Your financial situation and future expectations are essential in formulating an investment strategy. Before you decide on a particular investment to make, consider the following as they relate to your specific situation:

- Current and future income needs
- Need to provide for heirs
- Need to hedge against inflation
- Ability to withstand financial losses
- Security of principal and income
- Return rate
- Liquidity and marketability
- Diversification
- Tax and estate status
- Long-term versus short-term potential
- Amount of investment
- Denomination of investment (e.g., $5000 minimum investment, as required by some real estate investment trusts [REITs])
- Need for loan collateral
- Protection from creditor claims
- Callability provisions
- Risk level (high risk/higher reward versus low risk/greater security)

The Key Questions to Ask

You must always be open and inquisitive in personal financial planning. The answers you give for the following questions will significantly shape your investment strategy:

- What proportion of funds do you want safe and liquid?
- Are you willing to invest for higher return but greater risk?

- How long a maturity period are you willing to take on your investment?
- What should be the mix of your investments for diversification (e.g., stocks, bonds, real estate)?
- Do you need to invest in tax-free securities?

Sources of Investment Money

There are several ways of financing your investment choices. They include

- *Discretionary income.* After-tax income is disposable income, money available to you for spending or saving. You must commit much of your disposable income to fixed or semi-fixed expenditures such as housing, food, and transportation. Discretionary income is what is left after these expenses.
- *Home equity.* You may have a substantial amount of money in your home. You can cash out some of it by taking either a home equity loan or an equity line.

What Do You Want When You Invest?

If you want a safe investment with predictable but low return, invest in United States government securities, bank accounts, or money market accounts of mutual funds.

If you are retired, you may favor safe investments providing fixed yearly returns. In this situation, appreciation in the price of a security is not as important as stable, guaranteed income. Risky investments are undesirable, due to their uncertainty. For example, a retiree may be satisfied with a long-term government bond.

Two Investment Scenarios: What to Do

High Inflation. A rapid increase in inflation will cause interest rates to rise and bond and stock prices to fall. Avoid fixed income securities. However, the prices of precious metals (e.g., gold and silver) and real estate will increase.

- *Life insurance.* If you have a cash value (e.g., whole-life or variable life) life insurance, you can borrow up to a certain amount.
- *Profit sharing and pension.* If you own some form of annuity, you may borrow up to a certain amount at a low interest.
- *Gift*
- *OPM.* This acronym stands for "other people's money."

Warning: Be cautious in taking the advice of salespeople (e.g., brokers, mutual fund representatives), because their prime motivation is to earn a commission.

Investment return is affected by risk, liquidity, and size. Fixed dollar investments have principal and/or income amounts guaranteed in advance. Examples are bonds, preferred stock, United States government securities, and municipal bonds. Variable dollar investments do *not* have principal and/or income guaranteed. Examples are common stock and real estate.

Recommendation: Own a house, since you will likely enjoy appreciation in property value. If you rent, you are not building up equity. There is a tax deduction for home ownership in the form of interest and property taxes.

Are Your Investments Marketable and Liquid?

Marketability should be distinguished from liquidty. *Marketability* means you can find a ready market if you want to sell the investment. *Liquidity* means the investment not only is marketable but also has a highly stable price.

Liquidity may be important if you have limited investments or are saving for a specific personal or business item (e.g., down payment on a house). However, liquid investments typically earn less of a return than illiquid ones. Their advantage is that delays and transaction costs are minimized when you convert them into immediate cash. Liquid investments include savings accounts, money market funds, and certificates of deposit. If you may need funds in an emergency, you should have liquid funds!

Table 3.1 depicts marketability and liquidity factors for various investments.

Table 3.1 Asset Marketability and Liquidity

	Marketability	Liquidity
Savings accounts	Not applicable	Good
Money market funds	Good	Good
Corporate bonds	Good	Average
Municipal bonds	Good	Average
Short-term United States government securities	Good	Good
Long-term United States government securities	Good	Average
Common stock	Good	Poor
Real estate	Average	Poor

Depression.   Purchase long-term Treasury bonds. Interest rates will drop to close to zero, and you will have a safe security all others wish to buy.

After you have an emergency fund and funds to cover necessities, you may want capital accumulation. You will want an investment that grows consistent with your risk tolerance. In order to have growth, the after-tax return on the investment portfolio has to exceed the inflation rate. If inflation is high, your investment may not outpace inflation. Investments that typically provide long-term growth include common stock, convertible securities, growth mutual funds, and real estate.

EXAMPLE 3.1

You invest in a fixed income portfolio (e.g., bonds earning 9 percent). You are in the 28 percent tax bracket. Your after-tax yield is 6.48 percent (9 percent × .72). If the inflation rate is 5 percent, you have only exceeded the inflation rate by 1.48 percent.

You may borrow money to make investments. This is known as leverage. You can dramatically increase the yield on an investment otherwise made entirely from your own funds. This increase occurs when the return on the investment exceeds the cost of borrowing. You can maximize return by buying stocks on margin or by putting down as little as possible when buying real estate.

Income-oriented investments that provide continual cash flow include stocks paying high dividends (e.g., utilities), bonds, income funds, certificates of deposit, and Treasury notes.

As interest rates increase, stock prices decrease, for the following reasons:

• Dividends are less attractive so many people sell stocks and buy bonds.

- Buying stock on margin becomes more costly; this discourages investment.
- Financing becomes more costly for businesses; this means decreased profits and inhibited expansion.

The Impact of Economic and Market Factors

The following list shows the impact of changes in the interest rate on different securities.

Investments at Risk with Changing Interest Rates

Notes

Bonds

Mortgages

GNMAs ("Ginnie Maes," issued by Government National Mortgage Association)

Investments which Offset Risk of Interest Rate Change

Stocks

Real Estate

Gold

   General Rule of Thumb: Long-term interest rates on high quality bonds are about 3 percent more than the expected long-term inflation rate.

   This list shows the impact of changing economic conditions on various investments.

Investments Susceptible to Changing Economic Conditions

Bonds

Stocks

Mortgages

Real estate

Investments Not Susceptible to Changing Economic Conditions

United States government securities

Gold

Certificates of deposit

Investment susceptibility to market cycles is as follows:

Investments at Risk during Market Cycle Changes

Common stock

Real estate

Collectibles

Gold

Investments Which Offset Market Cycle Risk

Bonds

Certificates of deposit

GNMAs

Mortgages

Notes

Did You Consider a Mutual Fund?

A *direct* investment is when you buy a claim on a specific property. When you select an *indirect* investment, you invest in a

portfolio of securities or properties. One popular indirect investment is a share of a *mutual fund*, which is a portfolio of securities
issued by any one of several mutual investment companies.
Mutual funds are discussed in more detail in Chapter 7.

The Cost of Investing

You might want to take into account the investment expenses
associated with various investment instruments. Such expenses
do vary widely. The expense involved with a particular investment
is a relevant consideration.

Investments that require high expense include:

- Over-the-counter and inactive stocks
- Load mutual funds
- Unit trusts
- Zero-coupon bonds
- Limited partnerships
- Collectibles
- Certificates of deposit if withdrawn before maturity

Investments requiring low expenses include:

- Actively traded stocks and bonds
- No-load mutual funds
- Gold coins and bullion

Recommendation: Buy in volume to obtain discounts. For
example, as you increase the number of shares bought, the
brokerage commission per share drops. The greater the dollar
purchase of a Treasury bill, the less the commission. If you buy

a $50,000 or more Treasury bill from Merrill, Lynch, Pierce, Fenner, and Smith, there is a minimal commission. The smaller the purchase, the greater the per share commission rate.

How about an Asset Management Account?

Asset management accounts include checking accounts, savings via money market funds, investments (e.g., stocks, bonds) and credit cards. Monthly statements itemize all account and investment activity. Examples are Merrill, Lynch, Pierce, Fenner, and Smith's Cash Management Account; Charles Schwab's "One Account"; and Fidelity's "Ultra Service Account." Advantages of an asset management account are centralized bookkeeping, ability to write checks in any amount, and the automatic crediting of stock dividends and bond interest. Disadvantages are a high minimum to open the account (usually $5,000 to $20,000) and annual fees from $25 to $100. Also, some funds do not return checks.

How Inflation Affects You

Inflation is an increase in price for goods and services over a short time period. Inflation reduces the purchasing power of your dollar. The cost of living increases. For example, inflation can push up the price of housing so severely that many young adults cannot afford to buy a house.

You have to take inflation into account in making personal financial planning decisions. Adjusting for inflation involves the use of the "present value" and "future value" techniques. You must consider inflationary effects and interest compounding/discounting.

The Consumer Price Index (CPI) has more than tripled since 1967 (base year with an index of 100). From 1975 to 1985, inflation in the United States increased at an average compounded annual rate of 6.9 percent. Inflation has a negative impact if you have fixed-rate savings accounts or fixed-income investments (e.g., bonds), or are living on fixed income.

It's important to analyze your "real earnings," taking into account inflation and taxes. A change in "real earnings" may even be negative. In 1970, for example, the average wage earner made $119 a week. In 1985, the average weekly wage was $300. However, in terms of purchasing power, the 1985 wage bought only $110 worth of goods and services. This represents a decrease in "real" income of 8 percent.

EXAMPLE 3.2

You receive a 7 percent increase in salary. Your tax rate is 28 percent. The inflation rate is 4 percent. Your raise in "real dollars" after taking into account inflation and taxes is:

Increase in salary	7%
Taxes (.28 × 7%)	2%
Increase in salary after tax	5%
Inflation rate	4%
Increase in salary after tax and inflation	1%

Investments doing well or poorly in inflationary periods are given in the following list:

Good Performance in Inflationary Period

Common stock

Real estate

Gold

Collectibles

Bad Performance in Inflationary Period

Certificates of deposit

Bonds

Notes

Mortgages

Note: These fixed income securities decrease in value during inflation because they pay a fixed return.

Tip: In periods of high inflation, it's better to owe money, because you will be paying back in cheaper dollars. However, you will incur a purchasing power loss if you hold cash or are receiving fixed pension and annuity payments.

Determining Your Level of Risk

Personal risk means you may not be able to accomplish financial goals for one or more of the following reasons: death, disability, health problems, or casualties. Conservatism in financial planning is recommended, so that there is an aversion to high risk. Risk management includes consideration of: loss of life, property, and income; personal and professional liability; and medical costs.

Risk includes the chance of losing money on an investment. The more an investment can vary in value during the maturity period, the greater the risk you take when you buy and hold on to it. Questions to be answered regarding losses include:

- What potential losses exist, and what is the probability of loss?
- How much money will be needed in the event of a major loss?
- How much loss can be withstood, and for how long?

Aggressive versus Defensive Investing

Are you an aggressive or defensive person? Aggressive investment policies attempt to maximize profits and take above-average risk. Defensive investment policies are designed to reduce risk but also provide less return. If you invest aggressively, you tend to buy and sell more frequently. In a defensive strategy, there is a "buy and hold" philosophy. Aggressive investment may include buying securities on margin (credit) so as to increase profit potential. Defensive investment does not rely on leverage. Diversification is a defensive policy. Aggressive investing involves concentration—that is, investing in a few securities at a time in anticipation of a high return. (Chapter 4 in its entirety is devoted to issues of risk and return.)

The more money you invest in one source, the higher the rate of return. For example, a bank will usually pay you a higher interest rate on a $100,000 investment than on a $10,000 investment. Also, the greater your stock investment, the lower the brokerage commission per share. The more you invest in certain mutual funds (e.g., Fidelity Special Situations), the lower the sales commission will be.

Figure 3.1 shows the degree of default risk associated with different types of securities.

Caution: Be careful that obligations do not become so excessive that personal assets have to be liquidated as losses, to the extent that you may never recover from the financial effects.

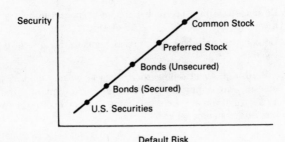

Figure 3.1 Securities and default risk.

Self-insurance may be suitable for small, manageable costs such as routine dental treatments. However, purchasing insurance is needed for longer, financially crippling situations such as medical problems, permanent disability, and death.

Some Investment Guidelines to Follow

- If you want to speculate, do it in stock, where the gains can be significant, not in corporate bonds.
- You are better off buying a high-quality bond issue than a low-quality one.
- Purchase stocks when they are undervalued and hold for the long term.
- Buy into a mutual fund that shows consistent long-term performance (e.g., over a five-year or ten-year period). A mutual fund may show great performance in one year only because of luck or unusual circumstances, or because the risky stocks bought shot up.

- Do not invest in a tax shelter unless it appears to be a good investment.
- Do not invest too heavily in precious metals, because of their volatility.

   Warning: Avoid selling short a stock, buying options, and investing in commodities. These are short-term investment strategies; if you are wrong on timing and market direction, you may suffer significant losses.

Conclusion

Your investment strategy will depend on your particular situation, including consideration of age, health, financial condition, tax rate, liquidity needs, and risk tolerance. You also have to take into account economic and market factors in formulating an investment program.

4

The Return
and Riskiness of
Your Investments

To be successful as an investor, you need an understanding of investment risk and realistic expectations of reward. An understanding of the tradeoff between the expected return and the degree of risk you must assume to earn it is perhaps the most important key to successful investing. This chapter discusses:

- Return and how it is measured
- Types of risk and how to reduce risk
- How to manage uncontrollable risk, using the concept of *beta*
- Investment alternatives and their relationship to risk

What Is Return?

Return is a key consideration in the investment decision. It is the reward for investing. You must compare the expected return for a given investment with the risk involved. The return on an investment consists of the following sources of income:

- Periodic cash payments, called *current income*
- Appreciation (or depreciation) in market value, called *capital gains* (or *losses*)

Current income, which is received on a periodic basis, may take the form of interest, dividends, or rent, among others. Capital gains or losses represent changes in market value. A capital gain is the amount by which the proceeds from the sale of an investment exceed its original purchase price. If the investment is sold for less than its purchase price, the difference is a capital loss.

The way you measure the return on a given investment depends primarily on how you define the relevant period over which you hold the investment, called the *holding period*. We use the term *holding period return* (HPR), which is the total return earned from holding an investment for that period of time. It is computed as follows:

$$\text{HPR} = \frac{\text{Current income + capital gain (or loss)}}{\text{Purchase price}}$$

EXAMPLE 4.1

Consider the investment in stocks A and B over a one-year period of ownership:

	Stock A	Stock B
Purchase price (beginning of year)	$100	$100
Cash dividend received (during the year)	$13	$18
Sales price (end of year)	$107	$97

The current incomes from the investment in stocks A and B over the one-year period are $13 and $18, respectively. For stock A, a capital gain of $7 ($107 sales price − $100 purchase price) is realized over the period. In the case of stock B, a $3 capital loss ($97 sales price − $100 purchase price) results.

Combining the capital gain return (or loss) with the current income, the total return on each investment is summarized below:

	Stock	
Return	A	B
Cash dividend	$13	$18
Capital gain (loss)	7	(3)
Total return	$20	$15

Thus, investments A and B offer the following returns:

$$\text{HPR (stock A)} = \frac{\$13 + (\$107 - \$100)}{\$100} = \frac{\$13 + \$7}{\$100} = \frac{\$20}{\$100} = 20\%$$

$$\text{HPR (stock B)} = \frac{\$18 + (\$97 - \$100)}{\$100} = \frac{\$18 - \$3}{\$100} = \frac{\$15}{\$100} = 15\%$$

What Is Annual Percentage Rate (APR)?

Different types of investments use different compounding periods. For example, most bonds pay interest semiannually; some banks pay interest quarterly. If you wish to compare investments with different compounding periods, you need to put them on a common basis. The annual percentage rate (APR), or effective annual rate, is used for this purpose and is computed as follows:

$$\text{APR} = (1 + r/m)^m - 1.0$$

where r = the stated, nominal, or quoted rate
m = the number of compounding periods per year

EXAMPLE 4.2

Assume that a bank offers 6 percent interest, compounded quarterly. The APR is:

$$\text{APR} = (1 + .06/4)^4 - 1.0 = (1.015)^4 - 1.0 = 1.0614 - 1.0 = .0614$$
$$= .0614 = 6.14\%$$

This means that if one bank offered 6 percent with quarterly compounding, while another offered 6.14 percent with annual compounding, they would both be paying the same effective rate of interest.

Annual percentage rate (APR) is also a measure of the cost of credit, expressed as a yearly rate. It includes interest as well as other financial charges, such as loan origination and certain closing fees. The lender is required to tell you the APR. It provides you with a good basis for comparing the cost of loans, including mortgage plans. For more on APR, see Chapter 9.

What Is Yield on Stock?

What is the yield being earned on your stock investment? It is the return for a common stock at its initial cost or present market value.

$$\frac{\text{Dividend per share}}{\text{Investment or market price per share}}$$

EXAMPLE 4.3

You paid $80 for a stock currently worth $100. The dividend per share is $4. The yield on your investment is

$$\frac{\$4}{\$80} = .05 = 5\% \quad \text{or} \quad \frac{\$4}{\$100} = .04 = 4\%$$

You can use the yield as an indication of the reasonableness of the price of the stock, particularly with stocks that pay stable dividends (e.g., utilities). Yield on stock is also a helpful figure if you are an income-oriented investor and wish to compare equity dividend returns with those of fixed income securities.

How Much Time Does It Take to Recover Your Initial Investment?

To compute the number of years to recover your initial investment, you can compute the payback period. (See also the section in Chapter 5 on the time it takes to get your money back.) Payback period equals:

$$\frac{\text{Initial investment}}{\text{Annual cash inflow}}$$

EXAMPLE 4.4

You invest $10,000 in a security that will pay out $2000 each year for eight years. The payback period is:

   $10,000/$2000 = 5 years

Note: The shorter the payback period the better, since by recouping your money faster you can invest it for a return. Also, a shorter payback period means less risk associated with recouping your money.

To determine how many years it takes to *double* your money, we employ the *rule of* 72. Dividing the number 72 by the fixed rate of return equals the number of years it takes for annual earnings from the security to double the original investment.

EXAMPLE 4.5

You buy a piece of property yielding an annual return of 25 percent. The investment will double in less than three years (72/25 = 2.88 years).

Calculating Growth Rate

You can determine a company's annual growth rate in market price, dividends per share, earnings per share, or sales, by using Table 2.1, "Future Value of $1," in Chapter 2. Of course, the higher a company's growth rate the better.

EXAMPLE 4.6

Company XYZ's market price of stock was $10 in 19X1 and $14 in 19X6. The annual growth rate is computed below.

$$\frac{\text{Market price in 19X6 } \$14.70}{\text{Market price in 19X1 } \$10.00} = 1.47 \text{ factor}$$

The number of years involved is five. Using Table 2.1, you find that the market price grew 8 percent over the five-year period.

EXAMPLE 4.7

Earnings per share for 19X1 equaled $.65 and in 19X6 equaled $1.00. The annual growth rate in earnings can be calculated as shown below.

$$\frac{19\text{X}6 \ \$1.00}{19\text{X}1 \ \$ \ .65} = 1.53846 \text{ factor}$$

Looking at Table 2.1 for $n = 5$ years and a factor of 1.53846, you find that annual earnings growth is about 9 percent.

A similar approach can be used in computing the growth rate in dividends or sales.

Types of Risk

Risk refers to the variation in earnings. It includes the chance of losing money on an investment. There are different types of risk. These risks affect various investment alternatives—stocks, bonds, or real estate—differently. All investments are subject to risk.

1. *Business risk.*   Business risk is the risk that the company will have general business problems. It depends on changes in demand or input prices and on possible obsolescence due to technological advances.

2. *Liquidity risk.*   This represents the possibility that an asset may not be sold on short notice for its market value. If an investment must be sold at a high discount, it is said to have a substantial amount of liquidity risk.

3. *Default risk.*   This is the risk that the issuing company is unable to make interest payments or principal repayments on debt. For example, there is a great amount of default risk inherent in the bonds of a company experiencing financial difficulty.

4. *Market risk.*   Prices of all stocks are correlated to some degree with broad swings in the stock market. Market risk refers to changes in the price of a stock that results from changes in the stock market as a whole, regardless of the firm's earning power.

For example, the prices of many stocks are affected by trends such as bull or bear markets.

5. *Interest rate risk.* This refers to the fluctuations in the value of an asset as the interest rates and conditions of the money and capital markets change. Interest rate risk applies to fixed income securities such as bonds and real estate. For example, if interest rates rise (fall), bond prices fall (rise).

6. *Purchasing power risk.* This risk involves the possibility that you will receive a lesser amount of purchasing power than you originally invested. Bonds are most affected by this risk, since the issuer will be paying back in cheaper dollars during an inflationary period.

Considerations in Deciding the Amount of Risk to Take

You have to consider the following factors in deciding the amount of risk to take:

- *Age.* If you are young, you can take more risk than if you are old. When approaching retirement age, you cannot take the chance of high-risk investments unless you already have a significant amount of safe earnings. If you are young and making a good salary, you can afford to take more risk to obtain significant wealth.

- *Occupation.* You should invest conservatively if you have uncertain or fluctuating earnings.

- *Family status.* If you are single, you can take more risk than if you have a spouse and child to support.

- *Personality.* If you feel uncomfortable with risk and will stay up nights thinking about your investments, do not invest in stock. However, some find a thrill in investing in stock.

- *Tax bracket.* If you are in a higher tax bracket, you can afford to take more risk when investing in securities, since the loss for the year (up to $3000) is tax-deductible.
- *Financial position.* If you have good net worth and liquidity, you can take greater investment risk.
- *Business sophistication.* If you are knowledgeable about the investment markets, you may undertake more risk.

How to Reduce Risk

Diversification is usually an answer to reduction in risk of loss. With a diversified portfolio (e.g., stocks, bonds, real estate, and savings accounts), the value of all these investments does not increase or decrease at the same time or in the same magnitude. Thus, you can protect yourself against fluctuations. One popular method of diversification is to own a share of a mutual fund, which is a portfolio of securities professionally managed by investment companies.

You can diversify in terms of maturity. For example, with securities of fixed maturity dates (e.g., bonds, one-year certificates of deposit), you can have maturities spaced so the securities do not all come due at once. Thus, new principal is available to invest periodically during times of high or low interest rates.

What Is the Risk/Return Trade-off?

Risk refers to the variability of possible returns associated with a given investment. Risk, along with return, is a major consideration in investment decisions. You must compare the expected return from a given investment with the risk associated with it. Higher levels of return are required to compensate for increased levels of risk. In general, there is a wide belief in the risk/return trade-off. In other words, the higher the risk undertaken, the more ample the return; and, conversely, the lower the risk, the more modest the return. The start-up phase of a high-tech company, for example, may involve high business risk. You would, therefore, require a high return on your investment in the company. In contrast, United States Treasury bills have very low interest rates, purchasing power, or market risk, which means a modest return to the investor. In fact, their average yield in the past 60 years has been 0.3 percent over the average inflation rate for the same period.

What Is the Meaning of Beta?

Many investors hold more than one financial asset. The portion of a given security's risk attributable to that security (called *unsystematic risk*) can be controlled through diversification. Business, liquidity, and default risks, which were discussed earlier, fall in this category. Nondiversifiable risk, more commonly referred to as *systematic risk,* results from forces outside of each firm's control and is therefore not unique to a given security. Purchasing power, interest rate, and market risks fall into this category. This type of risk is measured by *beta.*   **Tip:** A particular stock's beta is useful in predicting how much the security will go up or down, provided that you know which way the market will go. It does help you to figure out risk and expected return.

Most of the unsystematic risk affecting a security can be diversified away in an efficiently constructed portfolio. Therefore, this type of risk does not need to be compensated with a higher level of return. The only relevant risk is systematic risk or *beta risk,* for which the investor can expect to receive compensation. You, as an investor, are compensated for taking this type of risk, which cannot be controlled.

In general, there is a relationship between a stock's expected (or required) return and its beta. The following formula is very helpful in determining a stock's expected return, where the risk-free rate is the rate on a security such as a T-bill and the market risk premium equals the risk-free rate minus expected market return (such as Standard & Poor's 500 Stock Composite Index or Dow-Jones 30 Industrials).

Expected return = Risk-free rate + (beta × market risk premium)

Note: The market risk premium is the additional return above that which you could earn on, say, a T-bill, to compensate for assuming a given level of risk (as measured by beta). **Remember:** The relevant measure of risk is the risk of the individual security, or its beta. The higher the beta for a security, the greater the return expected (or demanded) by the investor.

EXAMPLE 4.8

Assume that the risk-free rate equals 6 percent and the expected return for the market equals 10 percent. If a stock has a beta of 2.0, its risk premium should be 14 percent:

$$2.0 \times (10\% - 6\%) = 2.0 \times 4\% = 8\%$$

This means that you would expect (or demand) an extra 8% (risk premium) on this stock on top of the risk-free return of 6 percent. Therefore, the total expected (required) return on the stock should be 14 percent:

$$6\% + 8\% = 14\%$$

How to Read Beta

Beta measures a security's volatility relative to an average security. In other words, it is a comparison of a security's return over time to that of the overall market. For example, if Paine Webber's beta is 2.0, this means that if the stock market goes up 10 percent, Paine Webber's common stock goes up 20 percent; if the market goes down 10 percent, Paine Webber goes down 20 percent. Here is a tip for how to read betas:

Beta	What It Means
0	The security's return is independent of the market. An example is a risk-free security such as a T-bill.
0.5	The security is only half as responsive as the market.
1.0	The security has the same responsiveness or risk as the market (i.e., average risk). This is the beta value of a market portfolio, such as Standard & Poor's 500 or Dow Jones 30 Industrials.
2.0	The security is twice as responsive, or risky, as the market.

The following table shows examples of betas for selected stocks (for more on beta, see the section in Chapter 5):*

Stock	Beta
	(1988)
Apple Computer	1.75
Exxon Corporation	.90
General Motors	1.00
IBM	1.05
Paine Webber	1.95
Reynolds & Reynolds	.95

* *Value Line Investment Survey*, New York, Arnold Bernhard Co., 1988.

Investment Alternatives and Risk/Return

You, as an investor, have a wide variety of investment alternatives available. These alternatives vary in terms of both the return they provide and the risks they carry. Table 4.1 summarizes major types of investments and their return/risk characteristics. The rankings assigned to each (none or low to very high) reflect the

Table 4.1 Investment Alternatives and Their Return/Risk Characteristics

Type of investment	Total return	Business risk	Liquidity risk	Purchasing power risk	Interest rate risk	Market risk
Savings bonds, savings accounts, money market accounts, CDs	Low	Very low or none	None	High	High	None
High grade bonds	Medium	Low	Low	Medium	Medium	Medium
Speculative bonds	High	High	Medium	Medium	High	High
Blue-chip common stocks	High	Very low	Very low	Low	Medium	Medium
Common stock mutual funds	High	Low	Very low	Low	Medium	Medium
Options and futures	Very high	Very high	Very high	High	Low–high	Very high
Real estate	High–very high	Low–medium	High	Low	High	Low
Collectibles	High–very high	Medium or high	Medium	Low–medium	Medium	Medium

authors' opinions. They should not be construed as absolute guidelines. **Note:** Each ranking is for a typical investment within the class, but there are many variations within each class.

Conclusion

Risk and return are two major factors you should consider in making financial and investment decisions. You must compare the expected risks and returns of each investment. Always remember that the higher the return, the higher the risk. *Beta* can help you estimate the expected return and risk of a security. In order to reduce risk, you might want to diversify your investment holdings by constructing a portfolio of different investments.

Part 2

Putting Your Money to Work

5

Should You Invest in Common Stock?

Common stock is an equity investment that represents ownership in a business (evidenced by a stock certificate which is transferable). For example, if you hold 3000 shares of XYZ Company, which has 100,000 shares outstanding, your ownership interest is 3 percent. Share means a fractional ownership interest in a firm. You obtain an equity interest in the company by buying its stock. As a stockholder, you can vote for the directors of the corporation. There is no maturity date to an equity investment. Your return is in the form of dividend income and appreciation in the market price of stock.

Although equity ownership returns vary with business cycles, stocks have shown over the years to be rewarding investments and good hedges against inflation. However, you should invest in stocks only if you have extra disposable income after building up sufficient cash savings for unexpected emergencies, life insurance, and other necessities. You should take into account your current financial condition: income, expenses, taxes, and future prospects for higher earnings. If possible, try to invest 15 percent of after-tax income in stocks.*

* According to the December 7, 1987 issue of *New York Magazine,* Americans save only 3% of their wages, while the Japanese save 22%.

Tip: Before you start to invest in stocks, your total assets should be two times your total liabilities.

Stocks are of two types: common and preferred. As a common stockholder, you bear part of the company's risk and share in its success. You may buy common stock on the listed exchanges or the over-the-counter market. Some general characteristics of common stock include:

Voting rights	Yes, one vote per share
Risk	High
Appreciation in market price	Yes
Price fluctuation	Yes
Fixed annual return	No, income varies with corporate income
Inflation hedge	Yes
Preemptive right	Yes
Last in bankruptcy to collect	Yes, common stockholders are paid after all others

You should be familiar with the following common stock terms:

- *Par value.* The stated or face value of a stock, this figure exists primarily for legal purposes. Some stocks are issued with no par value.

- *Book value.* This is an amount equal to the common stockholders' equity divided by the number of shares outstanding.

- *Market price.* The current price at which the stock can be bought or sold is the market price. Market prices are listed in the newspapers (e.g., *The New York Times*).

The Advantages and Disadvantages of Owning Common Stock

Among the benefits of owning common stock are:

- Voting right in company elections

- Share in dividends and increased market price
- Better hedge against inflation than with fixed income securities (if the total return from common stock investment exceeds the inflation rate)
- Preemptive right to maintain your proportionate share of ownership in the company—that is, to buy new shares issued before they go on sale to the public

Assume you own 5 percent of the company and there is a new issuance of 50,000 shares. You have the right to purchase 2500 shares.

On the other hand, there are some disadvantages to common stock ownership, including:

- Possible decline in market price
- Possible curtailment or elimination of dividends
- Receipt of dividends only after bondholders and preferred stockholders, in case of bankruptcy (thus greater risk)
- Possible forfeiture of dividends omitted in a year (which do not have to be paid in a later year)
- Greater price fluctuation than with fixed income securities

Types of Stocks

The type of stock you buy should be best for your particular circumstances and goals. The types include:

1. *Blue chips.* These offer ownership in high quality companies that are financially strong (e.g., General Electric). They have low risk and provide modest but dependable returns. They have good track records in earnings growth and dividend payments.

"Blue chips" are less susceptible than other stocks to cyclical market swings. A "blue chip" is for you if you want a safe, long-term equity investment.

2. *Growth stocks.* Companies evidencing a faster growth rate than other firms (e.g., high-technology businesses) and the economy in general are known as growth stocks. *Note:* Growth stocks pay low or no dividends, since earnings are normally retained for future expansion. While growth stocks usually increase in price faster than others, they may fluctuate more. A growth stock is good if you are planning to retire many years from now (e.g., in 10 or more years).

3. *Income stocks.* These are issued by companies having higher dividends and dividend payout ratios. These stocks are good if you desire high current income instead of capital appreciation. There is less risk associated with them. Income stocks are generally of companies in stable industries (e.g., utilities). Income stocks give you the highest income with stability to satisfy your present living requirements. They are attractive to retirees who depend on stability and periodic cash flow. **Tip:** You may be interested in income stocks when greater uncertainty exists about economic conditions.

4. *Cyclical stocks.* When a stock's price fluctuates based on economic changes, it is called a cyclical stock. These companies' earnings drop in recession and increase in expansion. The stocks are thus somewhat speculative. Examples are airlines and construction companies. A cyclical stock may be for a young individual who is willing to take risks and who is financially secure.

5. *Defensive stocks.* Stocks of companies that are basically not affected by a downturn in the business cycle are defensive investments. They are consistent and safe securities. However, a lower return is earned. Examples are utilities and consumer product companies. A defensive stock may be for an older person who prefers to avoid downward risk in the economy.

6. *Speculative stocks.* When companies without established track records issue stock, there is uncertainty regarding earnings but an opportunity for large profits. You may buy a speculative stock if you want a very high return and are willing to take high risk. Examples are biotechnology companies and mining stocks. Beware especially of "penny" stocks, which typically sell for less than $1 a share. Penny stocks are issued by companies with a short or erratic history of earnings, and thus are quite risky. Speculative stocks are for professional investors rather than the average person. Speculative stocks have high price-earnings ratios and price fluctuations.

A part of your funds should be invested in equity securities for diversification purposes. But do not put all your eggs in one basket; if all of your funds are in stock, you may suffer a huge loss in a stock crash. Do not forget "Black Monday," October 19, 1987, when the Down Jones industrials fell a record 508 points, or 22.6 percent!

Historically, over the long run, stocks have outperformed bonds.

What Types of Orders May You Place with Your Broker?

The types of orders you may place for stock transactions are as follows:

- *Market order.* You buy or sell stock at the current market price.
- *Open order.* Your order is kept open for a specified time period.
- *Day order.* Your order is good only for the day.
- *Good till canceled (GTC).* There is no expiration date to the order. It is open until the transaction takes place or is withdrawn.

- *Limit order.*   You agree to buy the stock at no more than a given price or sell at no less than a stated price. Your broker continues the order until a specified date or until you withdraw it. A limit order may be good to use when market prices are uncertain or fluctuate rapidly. The brokerage commission is usually higher on a limit order than on a market order.

EXAMPLE 5.1

You place a limit order to buy at $9 or less a stock now selling at $10. If the stock increases, it is not bought. However, if it decreases to $9, it is immediately purchased.

- *Stop-loss order.*   You agree to buy or sell a stock when it increases to or declines below a given price. **Tip:** Use this order to protect from further stock price declines by selling the shares at a predetermined price. **Recommendation:** Set a stop-loss order at 15–20 percent below your cost or the recent high. **Note:** Stop-loss orders are not available for over-the-counter stocks.

EXAMPLE 5.2

You own 100 shares of ABC Company at a current market price of $40 per share. You originally bought it at $25. You may place a stop-loss order to sell the stock if it drops to $35, to lock in a gain of $10 ($35 minus $25).

- *Time order.*   You ask your broker to sell a stock at a particular price in a given time period (e.g., month, week, day) unless you cancel the order.

EXAMPLE 5.3

You wish to sell 50 shares of XYZ Company at $40 per share. You believe the stock will rise to $40 in two weeks. You can place a

time order to sell the shares at $40, specifying a limit of two
weeks.

- *Scale order.* You give an order to purchase or sell a stock in
  specified amounts at specified price variations.

A settlement for a stock transaction takes place on the fifth full
business day after a trade has occurred. For example, if you buy
shares you must pay for them by the fifth business day (*settlement
date*) after the date of purchase (*trade date*).

An odd-lot transaction is one involving less than 100 shares
of a stock. A round-lot transaction involves units of 100
shares. **Tip:** If you buy fewer than 100 shares you usually have
to pay more per share for the stock, typically one-eighth of a point
higher; this goes to the specialist handling the transaction.
Further, the brokerage commission per share will come out
higher, because of the restricted volume. Brokerage fees per share
decline as the size of the order increases.

Your Dealings with Your Broker

Brokerage fees have to be paid when you buy or sell stock. The
brokerage fee generally ranges from 1.5 percent to 3 percent of the
transaction value. When you sell, you will also have to pay state
transfer taxes and a nominal federal registration fee. **Tip:** You
can save considerable money by using a discount broker if you do
not need full brokerage services. Table 5.1 compares the price of a
trade using a discount broker with the price of using a full-service
one. A full-service broker's services include preparation of research reports on companies and recommendations. Historically,
brokerage stock recommendations have not outperformed investing at random. Also, you may get a lot of "selling talk." **Note:** A
discount broker's fees typically range from 30 percent to 70

Table 5.1   Commission Schedule

Shares bought or sold	Market price	Representative full-service broker charge	Representative discount broker charge	Percentage savings
100	$60.00	$98.00	$49.00	50%
500	15.00	181.00	84.50	53
800	10.00	216.00	86.00	60
3000	25.00	879.25	209.00	76

percent of the fees charged by a full-service broker. **Flexibility:** You can also negotiate commissions with your discount broker.

Your decision whether to use a full-service broker or a discount broker depends particularly on the investment help and advice you need. If you make your own stock choices, you should of course select a discount broker.

Tip: If you are a heavy trader, try to get information from your full-service broker(s) and place orders with a discount broker. This way you can get brokerage house recommendations and at the same time pay low commissions.

How Do Stock Splits and Dividends Affect You?

Stock Splits

A stock split may occur when a company believes its stock price is too high and wants to lower the price per share to generate trading appeal.

Should you get excited about a stock split of a stock you own?

No. All that has happened is that you have received more shares; the total cost and value remain the same. Thus, the cost per share has decreased proportionately. While a stock split may positively affect the stock price temporarily, because of psychological factors and because it's now cheaper for others to buy because of the lower price, it does *not* change the underlying value of the stock.

After a stock split, your ownership percentage of the company is still the same. The market price of the stock theoretically should decrease on a relative basis for the split.

EXAMPLE 5.4

You own 1000 shares of Company XYZ at a cost of $10,000. If a two-for-one split occurs, you will receive two new shares for each old share. The cost per share will be halved. Theoretically, the market price per share should also be halved. After Company XYZ's stock split you will have 2000 shares at a cost per share of $5—still $10,000 in total.

Dividends

The two types of dividends you may receive are cash and stock. On average, United States companies pay out about 50 percent of their earnings in dividends.

Cash dividends are fully taxable to you and are typically paid quarterly. If a stock dividend differs in form from the security entitling you to the dividend (e.g., you own common stock but receive a preferred stock dividend), you have to pay taxes on the dividends received. If it is the same (e.g., you own common stock and receive common stock dividends), there is no tax on the dividends. Since the stock dividend becomes part of your asset base, tax is paid only when the stock is sold. **Recommendation:** You may wish to consider stocks paying stock dividends if you are in a high tax bracket.   **Tip:** Refer to *Standard & Poor's Stock Guide* for dividend records and ratings of companies.

Important dates for dividends are:

- *Declaration date.*   The date a dividend is declared by the Board of Directors represents a legal liability of the company.

- *Date of record.*   If you are a registered shareholder on the date of record, you will receive a dividend.   **Caution:** Do not sell your stock before the date of record, because you will lose the dividend.

- *Payment date.*   The date the dividend will be mailed to you is the payment date—typically several weeks subsequent to the date of record.

- *Ex-dividend date.*   This is four business days prior to the date of record. It determines who is eligible to receive the declared dividend.

A *cash dividend* amount is usually stated on a dividend per share basis (e.g., $.75 per share). It may also be expressed as a percentage of par value. Par value is an arbitrary amount assigned to a stock certificate as per the corporation's charter.

EXAMPLE 5.5

You own 10,000 shares of a company that pays you a cash dividend of $.50 per share. You will receive $5000.

EXAMPLE 5.6

You own 20,000 shares of a company's stock, which has a par value of $10. A 12 percent dividend is declared based on total par value. You will receive:

$$20,000 \times \$10 \times .12 = \$24,000$$

A *stock dividend* is payable in shares of stock. It is an issue of new shares expressed as a percentage of shares already held. For example, if you owned 500 shares before a 5 percent stock dividend, you would receive an additional 25 shares.

You really receive nothing of value with a stock dividend. You receive more shares, but the total cost of your investment remains the same. The cost per share drops; so does the market value. Stock dividends basically have a psychological rather than a financial value.

EXAMPLE 5.7

You own 1000 shares of ABC Company costing $20 per share, or $20,000. A 10 percent stock dividend is declared. After receiving the stock dividend, you will have 1100 shares. Your cost per share now declines to $18.18 ($20,000/1100 shares). If you later sell 200 shares of stock at $5000, your gain will be:

Selling price	$5000
Less: Cost 200 × $18.18	− 3636
Gain	$1364

Should You Take Advantage of Dividend Reinvestment and Cash Option Plans?

An advantage of a dividend reinvestment plan is that the company reinvests your dividends to buy more shares without your having to incur a brokerage commission. Further, you can often buy the additional shares at a discount price (e.g., 5 percent) from market price. You may want to identify those companies offering a dividend reinvestment plan by referring to *Moody's Annual Dividend Record*.

A drawback to dividend reinvestment is the delay in selling reinvested holdings, since the company typically holds the reinvested shares. Further, a company may not permit you to sell part of the reinvested shares; if you sell, you may have to sell all of your holdings to close the dividend reinvestment account. There may be a delay in buying stock through the purchase plan. Finally, reinvested dividends are taxable as ordinary income when paid, even though the distributions are not received in cash. Some plans also allow you to invest additional cash (above the dividend payment).

An automatic reinvestment plan is a form of "dollar cost" averaging: it allows you to buy stock during price declines as well as price increases, thus "averaging out" the purchase prices. **Recommendation:** Make a modest original investment in a company that offers a dividend reinvestment program and cash option plan. This allows you to invest additional monies without incurring brokerage fees and administrative costs.

Measuring Return on Common Stock

You can determine your return on an investment by computing the total dollar return, yield, dividend payout, and earnings per share.

Dollar Return

Your dollar return from a stock investment represents dividend income and change in market price.

EXAMPLE 5.8

You buy a stock for $30 and subsequently sell it for $36. The annual cash dividend is $2. Your return per share on the investment is:

Dividend income	$2
Gain ($36 − $30)	+ 6
Total	$8

If you owned 100 shares, your total return would be $800.

Percentage Return

What is the percentage return you have earned on your investment? It can be calculated as follows:

$$\frac{(\text{Selling price} - \text{investment}) + \text{dividend}}{\text{Investment}}$$

EXAMPLE 5.9

You invested $80 in a stock which you sold three months later for $90. A $2.50 dividend was received. The quarterly return is:

$$\frac{(\text{Selling price} - \text{investment}) + \text{dividend}}{\text{Investment}}$$

$$\frac{(\$90 - \$80) + \$2.50}{\$80} = \frac{\$12.50}{\$80} = 15.6\%$$

The equivalent annual return is:

$$15.6\% \times 4 = 62.4\%$$

EXAMPLE 5.10

You buy a stock for $60 and sell it for $100 after four years. Each year you receive a dividend of $3. The annual return from your investment over the four-year period is:

$$\frac{\dfrac{\text{Selling price} - \text{investment}}{\text{Years}} + \text{dividend}}{\text{Average investment}}$$

$$\frac{\dfrac{\text{Selling price} - \text{investment}}{\text{Years}} + \text{dividend}}{\dfrac{\text{Selling price} - \text{investment}}{2}}$$

$$\frac{\dfrac{\$100 - \$60}{4} + \$3}{\dfrac{\$100 + \$60}{2}} = \frac{\$13}{\$80} = 16.3\%$$

To get a relative idea of how you did, you can compare the return on your stock to the performance of a stock market index (e.g., Standard & Poor 500).

You can also calculate the return on equity of the company to see how well it has done. It equals:

$$\frac{\text{Net income}}{\text{Stockholders' equity}}$$

EXAMPLE 5.11

A company's net income is $1,000,000 and stockholders' equity is $10,000,000. The return on equity is 10 percent.

A similar version of return is:

$$\frac{\text{Earnings per share}}{\text{Book value per share}}$$

EXAMPLE 5.12

Company ABC has earnings per share of $4 and book value per share of $10. The profit rate is:

$$\frac{\$4}{\$10} = .40$$

Is the company earning a profit on its sales? Profit margin equals:

$$\frac{\text{Net income}}{\text{Sales}}$$

Dividend Yield on Stock

The yield being earned on your stock investment is the return for a common stock at its initial cost or present market value or inital cost.

Yield based on original investment equals:

$$\frac{\text{Dividends per share}}{\text{Investment}}$$

EXAMPLE 5.13

You paid $80 for a stock currently worth $90. The dividend per share is $4. The yield on your initial investment is:

$$\frac{\$4}{\$80} = .05$$

Dividend yield based on current market price equals:

$$\frac{\text{Dividend per share}}{\text{Market price per share}}$$

EXAMPLE 5.14

Assuming the same facts as in Example 5.13, the dividend yield equals:

$$\frac{\$4}{\$90} = .044$$

You can use the yield as an indication of the reasonableness of the stock's price, particularly when dividends are stable (e.g., utilities). Yield on stock is also helpful if you're an income-oriented investor who wishes to compare equity dividend returns with those of fixed-income securities.

Dividend yields are highest when stock prices are low, since dividend payments are less volatile than stock prices. A higher dividend yield is desirable. **Special Note:** The dividend yield on stock is usually less than the yield on a bond.

EXAMPLE 5.15

You purchased a stock at $30 paying an annual dividend of $3. Your yield is:

$$\frac{\text{Dividend}}{\text{Investment}} = \frac{\$\ 3}{\$30} = .10$$

What if conflicting signs exist between book value, price-earnings ratio, and dividend yield regarding your investment? Over time, dividend yield has proven a more accurate indicator of the future direction of the market.

The ratio of market price to dividends per share (inverse of dividend yield) indicates what investors are willing to pay for $1 worth of dividends. If the market price-dividend ratio of the Dow Jones Industrial Average goes below 18 (5½ percent yield), the market is considered undervalued, and an opportunity to buy exists. On the other hand, a market price-dividend ratio of about 30 (approximately a 3 percent yield) indicates an overvalued market—time to sell. Historically, the average yield of the stock market has been about 5 percent. An extreme variation indicates you should proceed with caution.

Dividend Payout Ratio

The dividend payout ratio equals:

$$\frac{\text{Dividends per share}}{\text{Earnings per share}}$$

A higher payout ratio indicates the possibility of higher dividends, pointing to higher stock prices. Over the last 100 years, the average payout ratio for "blue chips" has been about 67 percent. When the dividend payout ratios are much less than 67 percent, a possibility exists that the payout ratio will increase in the future. If you're an individual desiring high dividends because you rely on fixed income (e.g., if you are retired), you may favor a company with a high dividend payout ratio.

Earnings per Share

Dividends and market price of stock depend upon future earnings per share.

You can calculate estimated earnings at the end of the year as follows:

Estimated sales at end of year × after-tax profit margin

Estimated earnings per share at end of year are computed this way:

$$\frac{\text{Estimated earnings at end of year}}{\text{Estimated outstanding shares at end of year}}$$

How Do You Value (or Price) Stock?

In valuing your stock investment, there are several techniques you may employ, including book value, net current assets per share, price-earnings (P/E) ratio, and price-sales ratio.

Book Value per Share

Book value (net asset value, liquidation value) per share shows the amount of corporate assets working for each share of common stock. You may benefit by uncovering stock that is selling below book value or whose assets are significantly undervalued. A stock may represent a good value when its market price is below or close to book value because the security is undervalued. Companies with lower ratios of market price to book value have historically earned better returns than those with higher ratios.

Book value is based on historical cost, while market price is based on current prices. Thus, a stock may be undervalued relative to what the company is worth on the books. Because of inflation alone, market price should usually be higher than book value, since book value ignores inflationary increases. However, it should be noted that market price may be less than book value if the company is not doing well financially and/or has dim prospects.

Book value per share equals:

$$\frac{\text{Total stockholders' equity}}{\text{Number of shares outstanding}}$$

Total stockholders' equity = Total assets − total liabilities

EXAMPLE 5.16

You are thinking of investing in a company that has a market price per share of $40. Total stockholders' equity is $5,000,000 and 100,000 shares are outstanding. Book value per share is therefore $50. This may be a buying opportunity, since market price is well below book value and an upward movement in prices may occur.

Price-Earnings Ratio

The price-earnings ratio equals:

$$\frac{\text{Market price per share}}{\text{Earnings per share}}$$

For example, if the market price of stock is $50 and the earnings per share figure is $5, the price-earnings ratio (multiple) is 10.

The price-earnings ratio measures what investors are willing to pay for $1 worth of earnings. It shows stock price as a multiple of the earnings figure. It indicates the faith of the investing public in the company, and is a good measure of expectations (e.g., earnings) and thus value. The higher the price-earnings ratio, the greater the expectation of investors for future growth in the value of the stock. Conversely, a low price-earnings ratio means low investor expectations. Price-earnings ratios of companies are published in the newspapers in the stock quote section.

The following list shows price-earnings ratios of Standard & Poor's 500 Composite Stock Price Index.

1980	8
1981	8
1982	9
1983	12
1984	10
1985	12

How can you use the price-earnings ratio to value a stock? Estimated market price can be determined by:

Estimated earnings per share × estimated price-earnings ratio

EXAMPLE 5.17

You expect the sales for ABC Company to be $2,000,000, based on financial projections you read in a brokerage report and/or management's discussion in the annual report. The company's tax rate is 34 percent. The price-earnings ratio is 10. After-tax profit is therefore:

$2,000,000 × 66% = $1,320,000

Assume expected shares outstanding are $1,000,000.

Estimated earnings per share $= \dfrac{\$1,320,000}{1,000,000} = \$1.32$

Estimated market price = estimated EPS × estimated P/E ratio
$1.32 × 10 = $13.20

The price-earnings ratio is affected by a number of factors, including

- Growth rate in earnings
- Amount of future earnings and cash flow from operations
- Expected dividends
- Riskiness of company
- Instability in stock price and/or earnings
- Degree of competition
- Economic and political uncertainties
- Management ability

Price-earnings ratios vary from industry to industry and from company to company within an industry. The price-earnings ratio for a stock will also change with economic, industry, and company conditions. If a company's price-earnings ratio is much higher or lower than the average price-earnings ratio of other companies in the industry, you will want to know why! Historically, most large, stable, well-established companies sell at price-earnings ratios between 10 and 20.

Stocks in a given industry usually have about the same price-earnings ratios, and the ratios go up and down together. Companies in growth industries (e.g., computers) usually have higher price-earnings ratios than companies in established industries (e.g., utilities). Cyclical stocks usually have lower price-earnings ratios than companies that are stable.

A high price-earnings ratio is typically justified when corporate earnings are anticipated to grow. A high multiple generally means the stock market expects the company's future earnings to be higher than its current earnings. You must consider a company's current price-earnings ratio in terms of present and future economic and stock market conditions.

A company with a high price-earnings ratio may be an excellent company but *not* necessarily a good buy. The high price-earnings ratio may reflect exaggerated investor expectations. **Warning:** If you are a long-term investor, a high price-earnings ratio company should perhaps be avoided. If you pay a price that is many times higher than the earnings figure, the stock may have difficulty holding on to that high price. The stock would have to do even better than the "going" high expectations for you to earn a profit.

Suggestion: Examine P/E multiples for competing companies in a particular industry. This is a good starting point for researching what is happening in the industry. **Note:** The P/E ratio for a company may change over time due to changes in the financial health of the company and industry, as well as to other factors. The P/E ratio also reflects investor confidence in the overall stock market.

Tip: Also calculate a multiple for the stock market as a whole, or for a stock index. For example, a multiple for the Standard &

Poor's 500 can be arrived at as follows:

$$\frac{\text{Average market price per share}}{\text{Average earnings per share}}$$

Average market price per share equals:

$$\frac{\text{Total market price for all issues}}{\text{Number of issues}}$$

Average earnings per share equals:

$$\frac{\text{Total earnings per share for all issues}}{\text{Number of issues}}$$

A high price-earnings multiple indicates that investors view the stock positively. A low multiple indicates that investors look unfavorably on the stock, industry, or overall stock market. **Tip:** With a low price-earnings multiple stock, a short-term profit opportunity is unlikely. However, low multiples offer profit opportunities in the long term. **Suggestion:** A good time to buy stocks may be when multiples are lower than traditional levels. **Tip:** Spot a stock selling at a low P/E ratio that has good earnings growth potential. You have less downside risk and good upside potential.

EXAMPLE 5.18

A company's stock had a P/E ratio ranging from 10 to 20. This information was obtained from reading financial advisory service reports (e.g., Standard & Poor's), brokerage reports, or the company's annual report. The P/E ratio is now 11 (current P/E ratios of companies are listed in the stock pages of a newspaper), and the prospects for the industry and company are bright. This may be a buying opportunity.

The price-earnings ratio of a company may be distorted when a company has a very volatile earnings pattern. However, it is very difficult to attempt to normalize earnings to compute a meaningful P/E ratio. Instead of using the earnings per share for the last year, you may use average earnings for several years (total earnings/total years) or an average of past and estimated earnings.

Warning: Be careful not to rely too heavily on the price-earnings ratio, because stock market conditions, economic factors, etc. may outweigh the significance of the P/E ratio. **Special Note:** The price-earnings ratios for small or speculative companies and for firms with instability in earnings or no earnings records do not provide dependable data on which to base valuation estimates.

If your valuation of a stock differs from the price at which it is currently selling in the market, you may decide to buy if it is undervalued or sell short if it is overvalued. For example, assume Company XYZ's stock price is $40 on the market and your valuation indicates it is worth $50. The investment decision would be to purchase the stock.

How to Use Beta to Select a Stock

Beta refers to the percentage change in the market price of a stock relative to the percentage change in a stock market index (e.g., Standard & Poor's 500). Therefore, beta is a measure of the security's volatility relative to an average security. A high beta means a risky security. For example, a beta of 1.8 means that the firm's stock price can rise or fall 80 percent faster than the market.

Beta value	Meaning
<0	The security's market price moves in the *opposite* direction from the market. Very few stocks have a negative beta.

Beta value	Meaning
0	The security's return is independent of the market (e.g., risk-free United States Treasury security).
<1	The security's price moves in the same direction as the market, but the security's price fluctuates less than the market index. This is a conservative investment.
1	The security's market price moves in the same direction as the market index. The stock has the same risk as the market.
>1	The security's price moves in the same direction as the market, but the security's price fluctuates more than the market index. This is a risky security.

Many brokerage houses and investment services, including Merrill Lynch, Value Line, and Standard & Poor's, publish information on beta for various securities.

A detailed discussion of risk (and Beta) appears in Chapter 4.

How You Can Use Dollar-Cost Averaging to Your Advantage

You may take advantage of dollar-cost averaging for a stock you consider to be a sound long-term investment. This entails buying a constant dollar amount of a given stock or stocks at regularly spaced intervals—in other words, time diversification. By investing a fixed amount each time, you buy more shares when the price is down and fewer shares when the price is up. This usually results in a lower average cost per share, since you buy more shares of stock with the same dollars. Such an approach is advantageous when a stock price moves within a narrow range. If stock prices decline, you lose less money than you ordinarily would. If stock prices rise, you profit, but less than you usually would. However, dollar-cost averaging does involve greater transaction costs. **Note:** Dollar-cost averaging will not work when stock price continually drops. In general, dollar-cost averaging is a conservative way for you to invest, because it screens out "whims" which could result in buying high and selling low.

Among the advantages of dollar-cost averaging are the following:

- A conservative stock may be bought with relatively little risk, yielding benefits from long-term price appreciation.
- Buying too many shares at high prices is avoided.
- A bear market provides an opportunity to buy additional shares at particularly low prices.

EXAMPLE 5.19

You invest $100 a month in Company XYZ and have the following transactions. Assume no brokerage commission.

Date	Amount invested	Price per share	Shares bought
1/15	$100	$20	5
2/15	100	15	6⅔
3/15	100	12	8⅓
4/15	100	16	6¼
5/15	100	25	4

You have bought fewer shares at the higher price and more shares at the lower price. The average price per share is:

$$\frac{\$88}{5} = \$17.60$$

However, with your $500 investment you have acquired 30¼ shares, resulting in a cost per share of $16.53. At 5/15, the market price of stock of $25 exceeds your average cost of $16.53, reflecting an attractive gain.

The Time It Takes to Get Your Money Back

You can compute the payback period, representing the number of years it will take to recover your initial investment. Payback period can be determined by dividing initial investment by annual cash flow. See Chapter 4 for an example of how to calculate payback period.

What about Stock Valuation?

There are several ways to derive a valuation for a stock investment. These include time value computations, primarily determining present value; capitalizing earnings; and dividend-based values.

Time Value of Money

The time value of money is important for you to consider when evaluating stocks. Compound interest computations are necessary to appraise the future value of an investment. Discounting computations are used to analyze the present value of future cash flow from a stock.

Future Value (Compounding).   A dollar in your hand today is worth more than a dollar you will receive in the future because you can invest and earn interest on it. Compound interest occurs when interest earns interest. Future value indicates the worth of the investment in a later year.

Future Value of an Annuity.   An annuity is a series of equal receipts for a specified time period; an example is constant dividends. The future value of an annuity involves compounding, since the payments accrue interest.

Present Value (Discounting).   Present value computation is the opposite of determining compounded future value.

Present Value of an Annuity.   Constant dividends on stocks or yearly interest on bonds constitute annuities. To compare the financial attractiveness of financial instruments, you have to determine the present value of annuities for each one.

Common Stock Valuation

The value of common stock depends on the expected growth in earnings, dividends, and market price. Various methods exist to determine the implied value of common stock. One common method is present value computation.

The objective of valuing common stock is to ascertain whether the current market price is realistic in view of expected future dividends and price. The valuation process is directed at determining whether the stock is properly valued, undervalued, or overvalued.

The value of common stock can be determined by multiplying expected earnings per share times the price-earnings ratio.

EXAMPLE 5.20

ABC Company has an earnings per share (EPS) of $4. The expected growth rate in EPS is 10 percent. The normal P/E ratio is 8. The value of the stock is:

Estimated EPS = $4 (1.10) = $4.40
Price of stock = $4.40 × 8 = $35.20

The future market price of stock may be estimated using Table 2.1, "Future Value of $1," to determine expected EPS, which is then multiplied by the P/E ratio.

EXAMPLE 5.21

The current market price of a stock is $15 and the earnings per share figure is $1. Thus, the P/E ratio is 15. A 12 percent annual growth rate in earnings is expected over the next five years. Expected market price at the end of five years can be determined with the use of Table 2.1, "Future Value of $1," as follows. (Assume the P/E ratio will remain at 15 five years later.)

Current EPS × "Future Value of $1" factor for $n = 5$, $i = 12\%$
$1 × 1.76234 = $1.76
Expected market price = expected EPS × P/E ratio
$1.76 × 15 = $26.40

It should be noted that if EPS were expected to grow at a much lower rate (e.g., 2 percent), the expected P/E multiplier would be considerably lower than 15 because of the company's poor growth. Other variables besides earnings to be considered in valuing a company's stock are its total assets, net assets, and revenue base.

You can determine a stock's value by computing the present value of a security's anticipated future cash flows, using your required rate of return (the return rate you want to earn on your money) as the discount rate. The value of the common stock is the present value of your expected future cash inflows (from dividends and selling price). Value equals:

Present value of future dividends
+ Present value of selling price
  Value of common stock

Using present value tables, find the appropriate factor that corresponds to the rate of return (i) and the number of years involved in holding the security (y).

EXAMPLE 5.22

You are considering whether to buy a stock at the beginning of the year. The dividend at year's end is expected to be $2, and the year-end market price is anticipated at $50. The desired rate of return on your investment is 15 percent. The value of the stock at the end of the year (using Table 2.3, "Present Value of $1") equals:

$2.00 × .86957 + $50 × .86957 = $45.22

EXAMPLE 5.23

You want to estimate the worth of a stock. You anticipate holding it for 10 years and receiving $10 in annual dividends per share. The expected selling price at the end of 10 years is $40 per share. The required rate of return is 10 percent. The estimated value per share can be determined through the use of present value tables. The value per share is:

"Present Value of Annuity of $1" factor	$10 × 6.14457	$61.45
"Present Value of $1" factor	$40 × .38554	+ 15.42
Total present value of dividends and selling price		$76.87

If the stock's market price was $95 per share, you would not buy it, since that price is more than the $76.87 computed value based on your required rate of return.

EXAMPLE 5.24

You buy a stock with expected dividends growing at 10 percent, as follows:

Year	Dividend
1	$1.20
2	$1.32
3	$1.45

At the end of year 3 you expect to sell the stock for $20. Your minimum rate of return is 12 percent. The value of the stock today is computed using Table 2.3, "Present Value of $1," as follows:

Year		Present value (year 0)
1	$ 1.20 × .89286	$1.07
2	$ 1.32 × .79719	1.05
3	$ 1.45 × .71178	1.03
3	$20.00 × .71178	14.24
	Total value	$17.39

If the stock was selling today at $14, you would buy it, since it is undervalued.

Common stock valuation may also be based on capitalization of EPS, as follows:

$$\frac{\text{Earnings per share}}{\text{Capitalization rate}}$$

EXAMPLE 5.25

A company's future annual earnings is expected to be $2 per share. The risk rate of return (capitalization rate) is 14 percent. The value of the common stock equals:

$$\frac{\$ 2}{.14} = \$14.29$$

Internal Rate of Return

Internal rate of return is the rate you earn on your investment. This rate compares the present value of cash inflows to the present value of cash outflows. Assuming constant annual cash flows, internal rate of return is determined through the use of Table 2.4, "Present Value of Annuity of $1." You can compare a security's internal rate of return to the minimum rate of return you require, to determine whether the investment is attractive.

EXAMPLE 5.26

You invest $100,000 and will receive $20,000 per year for seven years.

$$\frac{\text{Initial investment}}{\text{Annual cash inflow}} = \text{factor}$$

$$\frac{\$100,000}{\$\ 20,000} = 5$$

Looking across seven years on Table 2.4 for a factor of 5, you find 5.03295, which is fairly close. The rate of return associated with this investment is about 9 percent. If the minimum rate of return you desire is 7 percent, you should undertake the investment.

If cash inflows from an investment are different each year, you should use the trial-and-error method, employing Table 2.3, "Present Value of $1," to derive a rate that results in the net present value closest to zero.

Importance of Stock Volume Figures

You may learn something by looking at the volume traded in a stock. For example, declining volume traded and a strong increase in price of stock indicates that buyers are more wary. Increased volume along with a drop in stock price indicates that institutions may be selling the stock. The situation is most positive when volume and price move together, when price rises on substantial volume.

It is generally best to trade in active stocks, because of readier marketability and less potential manipulation in price.

Should You Buy Stock on Margin (Credit)?

If you purchase stock on margin, you are buying securities on credit. Interest will be charged by your broker on the unpaid balance. The brokerage firm typically charges the borrowing investor 2 percent more than it is charged by the bank. A brokerage firm can lend you up to 50 percent of total value of stocks, up to 70 percent for corporate bonds, and up to 90 percent for United States Government securities. You have to put up more cash for equity securities than for bonds because of the greater risk involved. If the value of your portfolio declines enough to jeopardize the brokerage loan on your margin account, you will receive a "margin call" to put up additional money or securities, or sell some stock.

Buying on margin gives you the opportunity to improve your return through *leverage* (buying on credit). However, your loss can also be magnified, if the value of the security portfolio declines.

To open a margin account, you have to deposit a specified

amount of cash or its equivalent in marginable securities. Securities bought on margin will be held by your broker in "street name"—i.e., in the name of the brokerage firm.

EXAMPLE 5.27

You buy 50 shares of ABC Company at $40 per share, or $2000. You pay 60 percent of the price, or $1200, from your own funds, and borrow the remaining $800. Assuming an interest rate of 12 percent, the annual interest charge on the loan is $96 ($800 times .12). The brokerage fee is $50.

Buying on margin can result in a greater return, because you can make only a partial payment for stock that has appreciated in value. If the stock increases to $45 a year later, you can sell it for $2250 ($45 times 50 shares). Your profit before interest and brokerage fee is $250, on an investment of only $1200. The return rate is 20.8 percent.

Is an Initial Public Offering for You?

An initial public offering occurs when a company issues stock for the first time. Some new issues are offered by established, financially strong companies to obtain money or to go public. However, most new issues are offered by small, unknown, newly formed companies. Typically, they do not have track records. **Beware:** These companies represent speculative investments. But it should be noted that such new issues are potentially profitable, because these securities may have high returns in the *initial* period after the stock "goes public." On average, new issue performance is positive because the stocks are generally underpriced.

Your broker may call to make you a "special offering." Is he or she doing you a favor?   **Beware:** The brokerage firm may be trying to unload stock that professional money managers for mutual funds and institutional investors do not want. The retail broker receives a large sales incentive to push these shares. While no brokerage fee is charged to the buyer of such a stock (the seller pays the fees), it is usually a stock that professionals do not want!

Should You Venture into the Over-the-Counter Market?

The over-the-counter market consists of unlisted securities (those not listed on the recognized stock exchanges). The over-the-counter market involves broker/dealers who buy and sell securities through a communications network referred to as the National Association of Security Dealers Automated Quotation (NASDAQ) System, instead of on a trading floor. Unlisted securities are generally those of small companies.

Dealers keep over-the-counter shares in inventory.

Note: You have to incur the cost associated with the dealer's "spread" (difference between the price at which you buy shares and the price remitted to the seller), which can be quite significant.

Caution: Watch out for "penny stocks" on the over-the-counter market, because they usually have high risk and low quality. Some firms whose market prices for stock are in pennies per share may be headed for bankruptcy, while others may be new to the market and barely surviving.

EXAMPLE 5.28

Stock XYZ has "bid and asked" prices of $8 and $8½. This means that if you buy the stock you pay $8½, but if you sell the stock you receive only $8. Thus, the dealer's spread is $½. In addition, you must pay a brokerage commission on the purchase and sale.

You buy 1000 shares of XYZ and the brokerage commission is $150, your cost is $8650. If you then sell it immediately, your sales proceeds will be $7850 ($8000 minus $150). Thus you have to absorb $800, which is 9.2 percent of your initial cost ($800/$8650).

Should You Sell Short a Stock?

Short selling is used to profit from a decline in stock price. To make a short sale for you, your broker borrows stock from someone and then sells it for you to someone else. When the stock price falls, you buy shares to replace the borrowed ones. If you buy the shares back at a lower price than the broker sold them for, you earn a profit. You "sell short against the box" when you sell short shares you actually own (not borrowed shares).

You incur a loss with short selling, of course, when the repurchase price is higher than the original selling price. Significant losses are possible, since stock price may increase indefinitely. No matter how high it goes, you will have to buy securities to "cover," or replace, the borrowed ones.

To sell short, you must have a margin account with cash or securities valued at a minimum of 50 percent of the market value of the stock you want to sell short. While selling short normally requires no interest charge, you will have to retain the proceeds from the sale in your brokerage account. Of course, brokerage commissions will still have to be paid on the sale and repurchase.

Possible Reasons to Sell Short

- A decline in stock price is anticipated.

- You wish to postpone making a gain and paying taxes on it from one year to the next.

- You want to protect yourself if you own the stock but for some reason cannot sell (e.g., you buy stock through a payroll purchase plan at the end of each quarter but do not receive the certificates until several weeks later).

Guidelines in Short Selling a Stock

- Do not go against an upward trend in stock prices.
- If stock prices go up 10–15 percent, cover the short sale.
- Do not short several stocks at once.

Possible Times to Sell Short

- Officers of the company have sold a good part of their shares.
- Prices for the stock are volatile.
- Professionals forecast lower earnings for the company.
- The stock has "zoomed" up in a relatively short period of time.
- It is a "glamour" stock that is losing its popularity.
- It is a stock that has started to decline more than the market average.

Stocks to Avoid Selling Short

- Issues with limited shares outstanding
- Securities with a large short interest
- Stocks of companies that are candidates for takeovers

A disadvantage of selling short a stock is that you have to pay the dividends declared by the company to the person or firm from whom you borrowed the shares. Your brokerage firm will deduct the dividend from your account and place it in the account of the individual who lent you the shares. **Tip:** Sell short a stock paying low or no dividends.

Recommendation: Place a limit order rather than a market order when you sell a stock short. There is a danger in shorting a stock "at the market" since it can only be shorted on an "up tick" (that is, when the price is higher than the previous one). However, over-the-counter stocks can be sold short at any time. If the stock price falls drastically, it may be some time before an "up tick" occurs. For example, if a stock was initially at $40 when you put in your order, and drastically falls by the time it is sold short, the price may be $35. It would have been better to protect yourself against such a situation by putting in a limit order to sell, say, for $38 or better.

EXAMPLE 5.29

You sell short 100 shares of stock with a market price of $30. The broker borrows the shares for you and sells them to someone else for $3000. Subsequently, you buy the stock back at $25 a share, earning a profit per share of $5, or a total of $500 before brokerage charges.

The Proper Timing for Buying and Selling Stocks

Warning: Do not buy your entire portfolio at the top of a bull market when stocks appear very attractive with much good news. You may have to wait a long time for gains, because it may take years for the market to regain a prior peak.

Recommendation: Buy stock when prices are at very depressed levels and stock market and economic conditions appear gloomy. Stocks will then be selling for below-average price-earnings ratios. If you buy for the long term, chances are that corporate earnings and multiples will increase.

Of course, great uncertainty may exist as to whether the market is at a peak or bottom. No one can really predict accurately whether stocks will increase or decrease in price. **Solution:** To avoid buying your portfolio at a market peak, acquire a few securities at a time, staggering your stock acquisitions over months and years. **Tip:** Do not be fully invested in stocks for the amount of money you have reserved for investment. Keep some funds liquid for market declines, so you can take advantage of buying opportunities. Keep investing each year until your portfolio is diversified.

Buy a stock that no longer reacts negatively to bad economic news, since the news has already been discounted in its price. It probably will not decrease further.

If the price of a security is currently so high that it would *not* be a good buy, it may be time to sell. Selling should be done at one of the various phases of a bull market at the end of which a significant drop in prices may occur. In the last phase of a bull market, stock prices move above their intrinsic value and start to discount future possible events. Consider the following with regard to the Dow Jones Industrial Average:

Indicator	What to do
At three-year high	Sell stocks
At three-year low	Buy stocks

In timing the buying and selling of stocks, you should consider three sets of indicators: economic, monetary, and psychological.

Economic Indicators

Economic indicators apply to business outlook. A growing economy will lead to improved profitability and dividends; thus it is bullish for stocks. A decline in real gross national product will result in lower profits and dividends, causing a decline in stock prices. Buy stock when the economy has entered a recession—that is, when real gross national product declines for two consecutive quarters. Sell when the economy is growing at an unsustainable rate (e.g., a 10 percent annual rate for two quarters).

A low inflation rate is better for equity securities. During the "bull market" period of 1984 to 1986, the yearly percent increases in the Consumer Price Index were 4.0 percent, 3.8 percent, and 1.1 percent. Economic indicators can be used to confirm market direction. For example, if the economy is contracting at an unsustainable rate, stock prices will shortly do better, to reflect the better business environment that will emerge. Once the stock market does not react to bad news anymore, the market has already discounted the bad news and stock prices should start to move upward.

Monetary Indicators

Monetary indicators apply to Federal Reserve actions and the demand for credit. They involve consideration of long-term interest rates, which are important since bond yields compete with stock yields. Monetary and credit indicators are often the first signs of market direction. If monetary indicators move favorably, this is an indication that a decline in stock prices may be over.

A stock market top may be ready for a contraction if the Federal Reserve tightens credit, making consumer buying and corporate expansion more costly and difficult.

Good monetary indicators are:

- Dow Jones twenty-bond index
- Dow Jones utility average
- New York Stock Exchange utility average

Bonds and utilities are yield instruments and therefore money-sensitive. They are impacted by changing interest rates.

If the above monetary indicators are active and pointing higher, it is a sign the stock market will start to take off. In other words, an upward movement in these indicators takes place in advance of a stock market increase.

Psychological Indicators

Psychological indicators are important. If much emotion surrounds the market, then irrationality exists, and stocks are close to a reversal in trend. Psychological indicators apply to investors' attitudes regarding stocks. They include:

- Whether stocks are in strong (financial institutions') or weak (average people's) hands
- How much potential buying power is available
- Whether selling pressure has stopped
- Whether the market is behaving emotionally

Should You Diversify Your Portfolio?

Recommendation: To lower risk, diversify your stock holdings rather than investing in just one or two stocks and becoming highly vulnerable to stock price movements. Diversification reduces the volatility of your overall stock holdings. However, overall return will usually also be lessened.

Diversification may mean a stock portfolio includes growth stocks, income-oriented stocks, stable stocks, and speculative stocks. It is also possible to gain some diversification by buying a stock of a company that is itself widely diversified in its manufacturing and holding activities. Diversification reduces or minimizes your risk of loss. It is a defensive technique. **Recommendation:** Your stock investments should be made in 20 to 30 companies, so that if anything goes wrong with one company, a minimal loss will occur on the entire portfolio (see Figure 5.1).

You should diversify your investments over time so as to offset the ups and downs of the market. **Recommendation:** Avoid investing when the stock market averages are at new highs, and invest significantly when the averages are at new lows. **Note:** By investing more when the market is low and less when the market is high, you will be ahead of the game when the market is somewhere in between.

Diversification can be accomplished by investing in *mutual funds*, which are discussed in detail in Chapter 7.

What Kind of Stock Strategy Can You Employ?

As interest rates fall, stock prices rise. This occurs because less interest is earned on bank accounts and investors move money from low-yielding bank accounts to stocks. Also, low interest rates make it cheaper for companies to borrow, thus improving their profitability.

After you have looked at the financial data of the competing companies in the industry and determined that your company is the best value, then buy it. However, you should not necessarily buy a stock if everyone else is running after it, because it will become overvalued. You may be one of the last ones to get in on it.

Standard & Poor's Stock Guide has a stock rating system emphasizing earnings, dividend stability, and growth. An "A+" rating indicates the highest growth and stability of earnings and

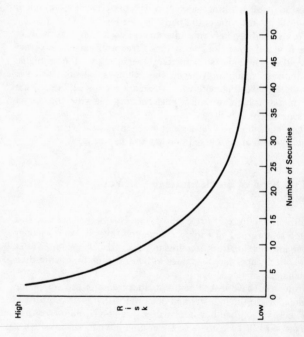

Figure 5.1 Diversification and risk.

dividends. A "C" rating signifies the lowest stability and growth of earnings and dividends. *Standard & Poor's Stock Reports* provide a brief interpretation of companies traded on the exchanges and in the over-the-counter markets.

In deciding whether to invest in a particular company, you should ask yourself the following questions:

- How is the company's cash flow?
- What is the capital spending of the company for expansion purposes?
- Is corporate debt excessive?
- What is the variability and growth in stock price, dividends per share, and earnings per share?
- Do earnings rise or fall in cycles?
- Is the company excessively regulated by the government?

Invest in quality companies (financially strong leaders in their fields that have had consistently high, profitable growth) and in the long term you should profit.

Buy an undervalued stock, which may be indicated by:

- A P/E ratio no more than twice the prevailing interest rate (for example, a P/E ratio of 20 compared to an interest rate of 10 percent)
- A market price of 20 percent or more under book value

Value may be found in stocks that are at new 52-week lows. Value may also be found in industry groups that have had a washout and are now fully neglected. The future may be good if the industry satisfies a long-term need, providing a necessary function or service. **Tip:** Make sure all the bad news on the industry is out.

One strategy for investing is to buy stocks with relatively low P/E ratios and high dividend yields. Some investors use the "7 and 7" strategy, according to which a stock is bought if the P/E ratio is less than 7 and the dividend yield is greater than 7.

A Word of Advice: In general, do not stay with an unprofitable stock too long if the future prospects are also poor. Take your small loss now before things get worse.

When the worst that can possibly happen to the stock market actually does happen, stock prices are bound to move upward.

An aggressive investment policy tries to obtain maximum profit by taking above-average risk. A defensive policy accepts lower profit because minimization of investment risk is desired.

Warning: Avoid concentrating investments in a few companies with high profit potential, because of the greater risk. If these few issues do not do well, significant losses may be incurred. **Recommendation:** Buy and hold a diversified portfolio of quality common stock for the long term.

Recommendation: Search out an industry that has had difficult times. Then pick and invest in a company with the best earnings record during the bad times. Since the company has done relatively well in tough times, it should also do well in good times, especially if better management comes in. Conversely, if a company has done poorly in good times, it will probably do much worse in bad times for the industry.

If a stock market index is very depressed (e.g., Dow Jones Industrial Average), and you notice that advancing issues begin to exceed declining issues for the first time, an upward trend may be occurring.

About two weeks prior to the end of a calendar quarter (e.g., June 30), buy high-grade stocks that have had a big move in the past 30 days. These stocks are being bought by institutional investors to enhance their reports. The upturn in those stocks should continue for a while.

Psychologically, one approach to investing in the market is practicing "contrary opinion." You determine what popular opinion is (based on emotions) and do the opposite. When an idea is in the minds of a vast number of investors, it is likely that the idea is based on emotions rather than on rational thought. **Tip:** When you hear only good things about the stock market or individual industries, watch out for a possible trend reversal. For example, when a great number of investment advisory services are bullish, this may be a bearish sign to you.

The Tax Implications of Your Stock Investments

Some tax rules you should know when you invest are:

- Dividends received are fully taxable.

- A capital gain occurs when the selling price exceeds the cost of stock you have held for more than six months. A capital loss occurs when the selling price is less than the cost of the stock you have held for more than six months.

- Net capital gains (capital gains less capital losses) are taxed at your tax rate. For example, if your net long-term capital gain in 19X9 is $15,000, the tax you will pay on it is $4200 ($15,000 × .28).

- Capital losses are allowed to the extent of capital gain plus up to $3000 ($1500 for married individuals filing separately) of ordinary income. The excess capital loss (over $3000) may be carried forward.

- Capital losses offset ordinary income. An ordinary gain or loss occurs on stock held for less than 6 months.

You must report your gains from the sale of stock on the trade date (date you sell the stock) instead of the settlement date (five business days later, when the broker must make payment to you). The settlement date may be in a later year.

Conclusion

When you invest in common stock, you must consider the risk-return trade-off. Your investment has to take into account your objectives, liquidity, tax position, risk preferences, need for steady income, growth potential, etc. There are numerous measurements of stock value you can use, such as the price-earnings ratio, discounted value of expected dividends and market price, and capitalization of earnings. Proper timing of buying and selling securities is also essential for your stock portfolio. If you invest right, your wealth will be maximized.

6

Should You Invest in Fixed Income Securities?

Fixed income securities generally stress current fixed income and offer little or no opportunity for appreciation in value. They are usually liquid and bear less market risk than other types of investments. This type of investment performs well during stable economic conditions and lower inflation. Examples of fixed income securities include:

- Corporate bonds
- Municipal bonds
- Notes
- Mortgages
- Preferred stocks

  In this chapter, you will learn about

- Basics of corporate and government bonds and the types of bonds issued
- How to calculate the yield on bonds and how to read bond quotations

- How to select a right bond for you
- Basics about preferred stocks and other short-term fixed income securities

What Is a Bond?

A bond is a certificate or security showing that you loaned funds to a company or to a government in return for fixed future interest and repayment of principal. Bonds have the following advantages:

- Bonds provide a fixed interest income each year.
- Bonds are safer than equity securities such as common stock, because bondholders are compensated before common stockholders in the event of corporate bankruptcy.

  Bonds have the following disadvantages:

- They do not participate in incremental profitability.
- There is no voting right associated with bond-holding.

Terms and Features of Bonds

There are certain terms and features of bonds you should be familiar with, including:

1. *Par value.* The par value of a bond is the face value, usually $1000.
2. *Coupon rate.* The coupon rate is the nominal interest rate that determines the actual interest to be received on a bond. It is an annual interest rate based on par value. For example, if you own a $1000 bond with a coupon rate of 6 percent, the annual interest payment you will receive is $60.

3. *Maturity date.* This is the final date on which repayment of the bond principal is due.

4. *Indenture.* The bond indenture is the lengthy legal agreement detailing the issuer's obligations pertaining to a bond issue. It contains the terms and conditions of the bond issue, as well as any restrictive provisions placed on the firm, known as restrictive covenants. The indenture is administered by an independent trustee. A *restrictive covenant* includes maintenance of (a) required levels of working capital, (b) a particular current ratio, and (c) a specified debt ratio.

5. *Trustee.* The trustee is the third party with whom the indenture is made. The trustee's job is to see that the terms of the indenture are carried out.

6. *Yield.* The yield is different from the coupon interest rate. It is the *effective* interest rate you are earning on the bond investment. If a bond is bought below its face value (i.e., purchased at a discount), the yield is higher than the coupon rate. If a bond is acquired above face value (i.e., bought at a premium), the yield is below the coupon rate.

7. *Call provision.* A call provision entitles the corporation to repurchase, or "call," bonds from their holders at stated prices over specified periods.

8. *Sinking fund.* In a sinking fund bond, money is put aside by the company periodically for the repayment of debt, thus reducing the total amount of debt outstanding. This particular provision may be included in the bond indenture to protect investors.

The Types of Bonds

There are many types of bonds, including:

1. *Mortgage bonds.* Mortgage bonds are secured by physical

property. In case of default, the bondholders may foreclose on the secured property and sell it to satisfy their claims.

2. *Debentures.* Debentures are unsecured bonds. They are protected by the general credit of the issuing corporation. Credit ratings are very important for this type of bond. Federal, state, and municipal government issues are debentures. *Subordinated debentures* are junior issues, ranking after other unsecured debt according to explicit provisions in the indenture. Finance companies have made extensive use of these types of bonds.

3. *Convertible bonds.* These bonds are subordinated debentures which may be converted, at the bondholder's option, into a specified amount of other securities (usually common stock) at a fixed price. They are hybrid securities, with characteristics of both bonds and common stock. Like other bonds, they provide fixed interest income; they also provide potential for appreciation through participation in future price increases of the underlying common stock.

4. *Income bonds.* On income bonds, interest is paid only if earned. They are often called reorganization bonds.

5. *Tax-exempt bonds.* Tax-exempt bonds are usually municipal bonds; their interest is not subject to federal income tax. Keep in mind, though, that the Tax Reform Act (TRA) of 1986 imposed restrictions on the issuance of tax-exempt municipal bonds. Municipal bonds may carry a lower interest than taxable bonds of similar quality and safety. However, after-tax yield from these bonds is usually more than that from a bond with a higher rate of taxable interest. **Note:** Municipal bonds are subject to two principal risks—interest rate changes and default.

6. *United States government securities.* These include bills, notes, bonds, and mortgages such as "Ginnie Maes." Treasury bills represent short-term government financing and mature in 12 months or less. Treasury notes have a maturity of 1 to 10 years,

whereas Treasury bonds have a maturity of 10 to 25 years and can be purchased in denominations as low as $1000. All these types of government securities are subject to federal income taxes, but not to state and local income taxes. "Ginnie Maes" represent pools of 25- to 30-year Federal Housing Administration (FHA) or Veterans Administration (VA) mortgages guaranteed by the Government National Mortgage Association.

7. *Zero-coupon bonds.* Zero-coupon bonds are bonds that make no periodic interest payments but instead are sold at a *deep discount* from their face value. Zero-coupon bonds are not fixed income securities in the traditional sense, because they provide no periodic income. The interest on the bonds is paid at maturity. However, accrued interest, though not received, is taxable yearly as ordinary income. Zero-coupon bonds have two basic advantages over regular coupon-bearing bonds: (1) A relatively small investment is required to buy these bonds; and (2) you are assured of a specific yield throughout the term of the investment.

8. *Junk bonds.* Junk bonds are bonds with a speculative credit rating of "B" or lower by Moody's and Standard & Poor's rating systems. **Be careful:** They are issued by companies without track records of sales and earnings, and therefore are risky for conservative investors. Since junk bonds are known for their high yields, many risk-oriented investors specialize in trading them.

How to Select a Bond

When selecting a bond, you should take into consideration four basic factors:

1. Investment quality
   - Rating of bonds

2. Length of maturity
   - Short-term (0–5 years)
   - Medium-term (6–15 years)
   - Long-term (over 15 years)
3. Features of bonds—call or conversion features
4. Tax status
5. Yield to maturity

Bond Ratings.   The investment quality of a bond is reflected by its bond rating, which measures the probability that a bond issue will go into default. The rating should influence your perception of risk and will therefore have an impact on the interest rate you are willing to accept, the price you are willing to pay, and the maturity period of the bond you are willing to agree to.

Bond investors tend to place more emphasis on independent analysis of quality than do common stock investors. Bond analysis and ratings are done by Standard & Poor's and Moody's, among others. Table 6.1 shows an actual listing of the designations used by these well-known independent agencies. Descriptions of ratings are summarized. For original versions of descriptions, see Moody's *Bond Record* and Standard and Poor's *Bond Guide*.

You should pay careful attention to ratings, since they can affect not only potential market behavior but relative yields as well. Specifically, the higher the rating, the lower the yield of a bond, other things being equal. It should be noted that the ratings do change over time and the rating agencies have "credit watch lists" of various types.   **Recommendation:** See if you can select only those bonds rated "Baa" or above by Moody's *or* "BBB" or above by Standard & Poor's, even though doing so means giving up about three-fourths of a percentage point in yield.

Maturity.   In addition to the ratings, the maturity factor can help you control the risk element. The maturity indicates how much

Table 6.1 Description of Bond Ratings*

Moody's	Standard & Poor's	Quality indication
Aaa	AAA	Highest quality
Aa	AA	High quality
A	A	Upper medium grade
Baa	BBB	Medium grade
Ba	BB	Contains speculative elements
B	B	Outright speculative
Caa	CCC & CC	Default definitely possible
Ca	C	Default, only partial recovery likely
C	D	Default, little recovery likely

* Ratings may also have + or − signs to show relative standings in class.

you stand to lose if interest rates rise. The longer a bond's maturity, the more volatile its price. There is a trade-off: Shorter maturities usually mean lower yields. **Recommendation:** If you are a conservative investor, select bonds with maturities no further out than 10 years.

Features. Check to see whether a bond has a call provision, which allows the issuing company to redeem its bonds after a certain date if it chooses to, rather than at maturity. You are generally paid a small premium over par if an issue is called, but not as much as you would have received if you had been able to hold the bond until maturity. That is because bonds are usually called only if their interest rates are higher than the going rate. **Recommendation:** Try to avoid bonds of companies that have a call provision and may be involved in "event risk" (mergers, acquisitions, leveraged buyouts, etc.).

Also check to see if a bond has a convertible feature. Convertible bonds can be converted into common stock at a later date. They provide fixed income in the form of interest. You can also benefit from the appreciation value of common stock.   **Note:** If you have only a small amount to invest or would like to have someone else make the selection, you can buy shares in one of the bond mutual funds. (See Chapter 7 for more about mutual funds.)

Tax Status.   If you are in a high tax bracket, you may want to consider tax-exempt bonds. Most municipal bonds are rated "A" or above, making them a good grade risk. They can also be bought in mutual funds.

Yield to Maturity.   Yield has a lot to do with the rating of a bond. The question of how to calculate various yield measures is taken up later.

How to Read a Bond Quotation

To see how bond quotations are presented in the newspaper, let us look at the following data for an IBM bond.

Bonds	Cur yld	Vol	High	Low	Close	Net chg
IBM 9⅜ 04	11.	169	84⅝	84	84	−1⅛

The column numbers immediately following the company name give the bond coupon rate and maturity date. This particular bond carries a 9.375 percent interest rate and matures in 2004.

The next column, labeled "cur yld," provides the *current yield,* calculated by dividing the annual interest income (9⅜ percent) by the current market price of the bond (a closing price of 84). Thus, the current yield for the IBM bond is 11 percent (9⅝ divided by 84). This figure represents the effective, or real, rate of return on the current market price based on the bond's interest earnings.

The "vol" column indicates the number of bonds traded on the given day (i.e., 169 bonds).

The last four columns indicate market price: the highest and lowest prices for which the bond sold that day, the price at the close of the day, and the difference between that figure and the previous day's closing price.

The market price of a bond is usually expressed as a percent of its par (face) value, which is customarily $1000. *Corporate bonds* are quoted to the nearest *one-eighth* of a percent, the quote of 84⅝ in the above example indicates a price of $846.25, or 84⅝ percent of $1000.

United States government bonds are highly marketable and deal in keenly competitive markets, so they are quoted in *thirty-seconds* or *sixty-fourths* rather than eighths. Moveover, decimals rather than fractions are used in quoting prices. For example, a quotation of 106.17 for a Treasury bond indicates a price of $1065.31 [$1060 + (¹⁷⁄₃₂ × $10)]. When a plus sign follows the quotation, the Treasury bond is being quoted in *sixty-fourths*. We must double the number following the decimal point and add one to determine the fraction of $10 represented in the quote. For example, a quote of 95.16+ indicates a price of $955.16 [$950 + (³³⁄₆₄ × $10)].

How Do You Calculate Yield (Effective Rate of Return) on a Bond?

Bonds are evaluated in regard to many different types of returns, including current yield, yield to maturity, yield to call, and realized yield.

Current Yield. The current yield is the annual interest payment divided by the current price of the bond, as discussed in the previous section on bond quotations. Current yield is reported in the *Wall Street Journal,* among other publications.

EXAMPLE 6.1

Assume a 12 percent coupon rate $1000 par value bond is selling for $960. The current yield is:

$1000/$960 = 12.5%

Warning: The problem with this measure of return is that it does not take into account the maturity date of the bond. A bond with 1 year to run and another with 15 years to run would have the same current yield quote if interest payments were $120 and the price were $960. Clearly, the 1-year bond would be preferable under these circumstances, because you would get not only $120 in interest but also a gain of $40 ($1000 − $960) within the 1-year period, and this amount could be reinvested.

Yield to Maturity. The yield to maturity takes into account the maturity date of the bond. It is the real return you will receive from interest income plus capital gain, assuming the bond is held to maturity. The exact way of calculating this measure is a little complicated and not presented here. But the approximate method is:

$$\text{Yield} = \frac{I + (\$1000 - V)/n}{(\$1000 + V)/2}$$

where V = the market value of the bond

I = dollars of interest paid per year

n = number of years to maturity

EXAMPLE 6.2

You have been offered a 10-year, 8 percent coupon, $1000 par value bond at a price of $877.70. The rate of return (yield) you could earn if you bought the bond and held it to maturity is:

$$\text{Yield} = \frac{\$80 + (\$1{,}000 - \$877.70)/10}{(\$1{,}000 + \$877.70)/2} = \frac{\$80 + \$12.23}{\$938.85} = \frac{\$92.23}{\$938.85} = \$9.85\%$$

Since the bond was offered at a discount, the yield (9.83 percent) would be greater than the coupon rate of 8 percent.

Yield to Call. Not all bonds are held to maturity. If the bond may be called prior to maturity, the yield to maturity formula will have the call price in place of the par value $1000.

EXAMPLE 6.3

Assume a 20-year bond was initially issued at a 13.5 percent coupon rate, and after 2 years rates have dropped. Assume further that the bond is currently selling for $1180, the yield to maturity on the bond is 11.15 percent, and the bond can be called in 5 years after issue at $1090. If you buy the bond 2 years after issue, your bond may be called back after 3 more years at $1090. The yield to call can be calculated as follows:

$$\frac{\$135 + (\$1090 - \$1180)/3}{(\$1090 + \$1180)/2} = \frac{\$135 + (-\$90/3)}{\$1135} = \frac{\$105}{\$1135} = 9.25\%$$

Note: The yield to call figure of 9.25 percent is 190 basis points less than the yield to maturity of 11.15 percent. Clearly, you need to be aware of the differential, because a lower return is earned.

Realized Yield. You may trade in and out of a bond long before it matures. You obviously need a measure of return to evaluate the investment appeal of any bonds you intend to buy and sell.

Realized yield is used for this purpose. This measure is simply a variation of yield to maturity and is derived by changing only two variables in the yield to maturity formula. Future price is used in place of par value ($1000), and the length of holding period is substituted for the number of years to maturity.

EXAMPLE 6.4

Refer to Example 6.2 and assume that you anticipate holding the bond only three years. You have estimated that interest rates will change in the future so that the price of the bond will move to about $925 from its present level of $877.70. Thus, you will buy the bond today at a market price of $877.70 and sell the issue three years later at a price of $925. Given these assumptions, the realized yield of this bond would be

$$\text{Realized yield} = \frac{\$80 + (\$925 - \$877.70)/3}{(\$925 + \$877.70)/2} =$$

$$\frac{\$80 + \$15.77}{\$901.35} = \frac{\$95.77}{\$901.35} = 10.63\%$$

Note: You can use a bond table to find the value for various yield measures. A source is *Thorndike Encyclopedia of Banking and Financial Tables* by Warren, Gorham & Lamont, Boston.

Equivalent Before-Tax Yield.   Yield on a municipal bond needs to be looked at on an equivalent before-tax yield basis, because the interest received is not subject to federal income taxes. The formula used to equate interest on municipals with interest on other investments is:

$$\text{Tax equivalent yield} = \text{tax-exempt yield}/(1 - \text{tax rate})$$

EXAMPLE 6.5

If you have a marginal tax rate of 28 percent and are evaluating a municipal bond paying 10 percent interest, the equivalent before-tax yield on a taxable investment would be:

$$10\%/(1 - .28) = 13.9\%$$

Thus, you could choose between a taxable investment paying 13.9 percent and a tax-exempt bond paying 10 percent, since the two investments would be equivalent.

What Is Preferred Stock?

Preferred stock carries a fixed dividend that is paid quarterly. The dividend is stated in dollar terms per share, or as a percentage of par (stated) value of the stock. Preferred stock is considered a hybrid security because it possesses features of both common stock and a corporate bond. It is like common stock in that:

- It represents equity ownership and is issued without stated maturity dates.
- It pays dividends.

Preferred stock is also like a corporate bond in that:

- It provides for prior claims on earnings and assets.
- Its dividend is fixed for the life of the issue.
- It can carry call and convertible features and sinking fund provisions.

Since preferred stocks are traded on the basis of the yield offered to investors, they are in effect viewed as fixed income securities and, as a result, are in competition with bonds in the marketplace.   **Note:** Corporate bonds, however, occupy a position senior to preferred stocks.

Advantages of owning preferred stocks include:

- High current income, which is highly predictable
- Safety
- Lower unit cost ($10 to $25 per share)

Disadvantages of preferred stocks are:

- Susceptibility to inflation and high interest rates
- Lack of substantial capital gains potential

Preferred Stock Ratings

Standard & Poor's and Moody's have long rated the investment quality of preferred stocks as well as of bonds. S&P uses basically the same rating system for preferred stocks as for bonds, except that triple A ratings are not given to preferred stocks. Moody's uses a slightly different system, which is given in Table 6.2. These

Table 6.2   Moody's Preferred Stock Rating System

Rating symbol	Definition
aaa	Top quality
aa	High grade
a	Upper medium grade
baa	Lower medium grade
ba	Speculative type
b	Little assurance of future dividends
caa	Likely to be already in arrears

ratings are intended to provide an indication of the quality of the issue and are based largely on an assessment of the firm's ability to pay preferred dividends in a prompt and timely fashion. **Note:** Preferred stock ratings should not be compared with bond ratings, as they are not equivalent; preferred stocks occupy a position junior to bonds.

How to Calculate Expected Return from Preferred Stock

The expected return from preferred stock is calculated in the same way as the expected return on bonds. Since preferred stock usually has no maturity date when the company must redeem it, you cannot calculate a yield to maturity. You can calculate a current yield, as follows:

Current yield $= D/P$

where D = annual dividend
P = the market price of the preferred stock

EXAMPLE 6.6

A preferred stock paying $4 a year in dividends and having a market price of $25 would have a current yield of 16 percent ($4/$25).

Preferred Stock Quotations

If preferred stocks are listed on the organized exchanges, they are reported in the same sections as common stocks in newspapers. The symbol "pf" appears after the name of the corporation, designating the issue as preferred. Preferred stock quotations are read the same way as common stock quotations. The issues are listed in *Moody's Bond Record.*

Other Fixed Income Securities— Short-Term "Parking Lots"

Besides bonds and preferred stock, there are other significant forms of debt instruments which are primarily *short-term* in nature. You may treat them as "parking lots" for your money until you decide what the next investment should be.

- *Certificates of deposit (CDs).* These safe instruments are issued by commercial banks and thrift institutions and have traditionally been in amounts of $10,000 or $100,000 (jumbo CDs). You can invest in a CD for much less (e.g., $2000, $5000). CDs have a fixed maturity period, varying from several months to many years. **Warning:** There is a penalty for cashing in the certificate prior to the maturity date, however.
- *Commercial paper.* Commercial paper is issued by large corporations to the public. Unfortunately, it usually comes in minimum denominations of $25,000. It represents an unsecured promissory note. It usually carries a higher yield than small CDs. The maturity is usually 30, 60, or 90 days. The degree of risk depends on the company's credit rating.
- *Treasury bills.* Treasury bills have a maximum maturity of one year and common maturities of 91 and 182 days. They trade in minimum units of $10,000. They do not pay interest in the traditional sense; they are sold at a discount, and redeemed at face value when the maturity date comes around. T-bills are extremely liquid, in that there is an active secondary or resale market for

these securities. T-bills have an extremely low risk because they are backed by the United States government.

• *Money market funds.* The money market fund is a special form of mutual fund. You can own a portfolio of high-yielding CDs, T-bills, and other similar securities of short-term nature, even if you have only a small amount to invest. There is a great deal of liquidity and flexibility in withdrawing funds through check-writing privileges (the usual minimum withdrawal is $500). Money market funds are considered very conservative, because most of the securities purchased by the funds are quite safe. For more about money market funds, refer to Chapter 7.

Conclusion

Fixed income securities such a bonds and preferred stocks have a twofold appeal to investors: They are usually safer than equity securities, such as common stocks, and they typically generate a higher current return. It is important to realize that yields and prices of bonds can be just as volatile as common stock prices, and almost as risky. Bonds are subject to default risk, interest rate risk, and inflation risk. Preferred stock is a hybrid security, since it has features of both common stock and bonds. Investing in fixed income securities requires an understanding of quality ratings and risks associated with the securities.

7

Should You Invest in a Mutual Fund?

If you are an investor interested in receiving the benefit of professional portfolio management but do not have sufficient funds to purchase a diversified mix of securities, you will find the purchase of mutual fund shares very attractive. In this chapter you will learn about the following:

- Special features and advantages of investing in mutual funds
- How to evaluate the performance of a mutual fund
- Types of funds and how they fit into your investment goals
- Special types of funds, such as money market funds and bond funds
- How to read mutual fund quotations
- How to calculate your real return on mutual fund investments
- What beta means in terms of risk of a fund
- What factors to consider in selecting a mutual fund

The Special Features of Mutual Fund Investing

Mutual funds are popular investment vehicles that offer ownership of a professionally managed portfolio of securities. Major advantages of investing in mutual funds are:

1. *Diversification.*   Each share of a fund gives you an interest in a cross-section of stocks, bonds, or other investments.

2. *Small minimum investment.*   You can achieve diversification with a small amount of money (as little as $25 or $50) through the large number of securities in the portfolio. A handful of funds have no minimums.

3. *Automatic reinvestment.*   Most funds allow you automatically to reinvest dividends and any capital gains which may arise from the fund's buying and selling activities. Funds typically do not charge a sales fee on automatic reinvestments.

4. *Automatic withdrawals.*   Most funds will allow you to withdraw money on a regular basis.

5. *Liquidity.*   You are allowed to redeem the shares you own.

6. *Switching.*   You may want to make changes in your investments. Your long-term goals may remain the same, but the investment climate does not. To facilitate switching among funds, companies such as Fidelity and Vanguard have introduced "families" of funds. You may move your investment among them with relative freedom, usually at no fee.

What Is Net Asset Value (NAV)?

The value of a mutual fund share is measured by net asset value (NAV), which equals

$$\frac{\text{Fund's total assets} - \text{liabilities}}{\text{Number of shares outstanding in the fund}}$$

EXAMPLE 7.1

For simplicity, assume that a fund owns 100 shares each of GM, Xerox, and IBM. Assume also that on a particular day, the market values of these shares are as follows. The NAV of the fund is calculated this way (assume the fund has no liabilities):

(a) GM—$90 per share × 100 shares	$ 9,000
(b) Xerox—$100 per share × 100 shares	10,000
(c) IBM—$160 per share × 100 shares	16,000
(d) Value of the fund's portfolio	$35,000
(e) Number of shares outstanding in the fund	1,000
(f) Net asset value (NAV) per share = (d)/(e)	$ 35

If you own 5 percent of the fund's outstanding shares, or 50 shares (5 percent of 1000 shares), then the value of your investment is $1750 ($35 times 50).

How Do You Make Money in a Mutual Fund?

There are three ways to make money in mutual funds. NAV is only one of the three. You also receive capital gains and dividends.

Most investors grew up on stocks and are used to simply looking at a price in the paper. **Warning:** For evaluating stock performance this is perfectly OK, but it's not for mutual funds. Do not just look at the NAV in the paper. That indicates only the current market value of the underlying portfolio. **Tip:** Be sure to know how many shares you have in order to figure out the total value of your holdings. Chances are, anyone in a fund for more than several months has more shares than when he or she started. This is because most funds pay dividends and capital gains distributions, which are usually reinvested automatically in the form of additional shares.

To get a good feel for how many shares of a fund you own, look at your most recent statement from the fund company. By multiplying the number of shares by the net asset value per share, you can come up with a more accurate picture of how much money you have actually made.

EXAMPLE 7.2

Take a 10-year investment in T. Rowe Price's New Horizon Fund. $1000 invested in 1976 would have been worth more than $4400, a 342 percent total return, at the end of 1986. But nearly two-thirds of those gains came from capital gains and dividends. Just looking at net asset value would have revealed only a 69 percent return.

Note: A more accurate way of calculating your personal rate of return in a mutual fund will be discussed in a future section of this chapter ("Performance of Mutual Funds").

The Types of Mutual Funds

Mutual funds may be classified into different types, according to kinds of organization, fees charged, methods of trading funds, and investment objectives. With *open-end* funds, you buy from and sell shares back to the fund itself. On the other hand, *closed-end* funds operate with a fixed number of shares outstanding which trade among individuals in secondary markets, as do common stocks. All open-end and closed-end funds charge management fees. A major feature of closed-end funds is the size of discount or premium—that is, the difference between their market prices and their net asset values (NAVs). Many funds of this type sell at discounts; this enhances their investment appeal.

Funds that charge sales commissions are called *load* funds. *No-load funds* do not charge sales commissions. Their sales strategies include advertisements and (800) WATS-line telephone orders.

Tip: Load funds perform no better than no-load funds. Many experts believe you should buy only no-load or low-load funds. You should have no trouble finding funds of those types that meet your investment requirements.

Note: If you are interested in investing in mutual funds, obtain and study closely the prospectus of each fund you're considering, in order to select a fund meeting your investment goals and tolerance for risk. The prospectus contains such information as the fund's investment objective, method of selecting securities, performance figures, sales charges, and other expenses.

Depending on their investment philosophies, mutual funds generally fall into ten major categories.

1. *Money market funds.* Money market funds invest exclusively in debt securities maturing within one year, such as government securities, commercial paper, and certificates of deposit. These funds provide a safety valve for you because the price never changes. They are known as dollar funds, which means you always buy and sell shares at $1 each.

2. *Aggressive growth funds.* Aggressive growth funds go for big future capital gains instead of current dividend income. They invest in the stocks of upstart and high-tech-oriented companies. Return can be great—but so can risk. These funds are for you only if you are not particularly concerned with short-term fluctuations in return but seek long-term gains. Aggressive growth funds are

also called *maximum capital gain, capital appreciation,* and *small-company growth funds.*

3. *Growth funds.* Growth funds seek long-term gains by investing in the stocks of established companies which are expected to rise in value faster than inflation. These stocks are best for you if you desire steady growth over a long-term period but feel little need for income in the meantime.

4. *Income funds.* Income funds are best for you if you seek a high level of dividend income. Income funds usually invest in high-quality bonds and stocks with consistently high dividends.

5. *Growth and income funds.* Growth and income funds seek both current dividend income and capital gains. The goal of these funds is to provide long-term growth without much variation in share value.

6. *Balanced funds.* Balanced funds combine investments in common stock, bonds, and, often, preferred stock. They attempt to provide income and some capital appreciation. Balanced funds tend to underperform all-stock funds in strong bull markets.

7. *Bond and preferred stock funds.* These funds invest in both bonds and preferred stock, with the emphasis on income rather than growth. The funds that invest exclusively in bonds are called *bond funds.* There are two types of bond funds: funds that invest in *corporate bonds,* and *municipal bond funds* that provide tax-free income and a diversified portfolio of municipal securities. In periods of volatile interest rates, bond funds are subject to price fluctuations. The value of the shares will fall when interest rates rise.

8. *Index funds.* Index funds invest in a portfolio of corporate stocks, the composition of which is determined by the Standard & Poor's 500 or some other market index.

9. *Sector funds.* Sector funds invest in one or two fields or industries. These funds are risky in that they rise and fall

depending on how the individual fields or industries do. They are also called *specialized funds*.

10. *International funds.* International funds invest in the stocks and bonds of corporations traded on foreign exchanges. These funds make significant gains when the dollar is falling and foreign stock prices are rising.

More about Money Market Funds

Money market mutual funds invest in short-term government securities, commercial paper, and certificates of deposit. They provide more safety of principal than other mutual funds, since net asset value never fluctuates. Each share has a net asset value of $1. The yield, however, fluctuates daily.

Here are the major advantages of money market funds:

- Money market funds are no-load.
- A minimum deposit in these funds can be as little as $1000
- The fund is a form of checking account, allowing you to write checks against your balance in the account. The usual minimum withdrawal is $500.
- You earn interest daily.
- You can use these funds as a "parking place" in which to put money while waiting to make another investment.

Disadvantage: Your deposit in these funds is not insured, as it is in a money market account or other federally insured deposit in banks.

Recommendation: If you are in a high tax bracket, consider a fund that invests in tax-free municipal bonds.

What You Need to Know about a Bond Fund

There are three key facts you should know about the bonds in any portfolio. If you cannot find these facts in the fund's annual report or prospectus, phone the fund and get the answers directly.

• *Quality.*   Check the credit rating of the typical bond in your fund. Ratings by Standard & Poor's and Moody's show the relative danger that an issuer will default on interest or principal payments. "AAA" is the best grade.   **Note:** A rating of "BB" or lower signifies a junk bond.

• *Maturity.*   The average maturity of your fund's bonds indicates how much you stand to lose if interest rates rise. The longer the term of a bond, the more volatile its price. For example, a 20-year bond may fluctuate in price four times as much as a four-year issue.

• *Premium or discount.*   Some funds with high current yields hold bonds that trade for more than their face value, or at a premium. Such funds are less vulnerable to losses if rates go up. Funds holding bonds that trade at a discount to face value can lose most.

You must keep in mind the following guidelines:

• Rising interest rates drive down the value of all bond funds. Rather than focusing only on current yield, therefore, you should look primarily at total return (yield plus capital gains from falling interest rates, or minus capital losses if rates climb).

• All bond funds do not benefit equally from tumbling interest rates.   **Tip:** If you think interest rates will decline and you want to increase your total return, buy funds that invest in United States Treasuries or top-rated corporate bonds. Consider high-yield corporate bonds (junk bonds) if you believe rates are stabilizing.

• Unlike bonds, bond funds do not allow you to lock in a yield. A mutual fund with a constantly changing portfolio is not like an individual bond, which you can keep to maturity. If you want steady, secure income over several years or more, consider, as alternatives to funds, buying individual top-quality bonds or investing in a municipal bond unit trust, which maintains a fixed portfolio.

How to Read Mutual Fund Quotations

Below are quotations of mutual funds shown in a newspaper.

Funds	NAV	Offer price	NAV chg.
Acorn Fund	30.95	N.L.	+.38
. . .	. . .	. . .	. . .
American Growth	8.52	9.31	+.05

In a *load fund,* the price you pay for a share is called the *offer price,* and it is higher than net asset value (NAV), the difference being the commission. As shown above, American Growth has a load of $0.79 ($9.31 − $8.52), or 8.49 percent ($0.79/$9.31). Acorn Fund is a *no-load* fund, as "N.L." indicates. In a no-load fund, the price you pay is the NAV.

Below is a typical listing of *closed-end* funds shown in a newspaper.

Funds	NAV	Strike price	% diff
Claremont	35.92	29⅜	−18.2
. . .	. . .	. . .	. . .
Nautilus	34.41	34½	+ 0.2

In "% diff" column, negative difference means the shares sell at a discount; positive difference means they sell at a premium.

Performance of Mutual Funds

Generally, mutual funds provide returns to you in the form of (1) dividend income, (2) capital gain distribution, and (3) change in capital (or NAV) of the fund. **Remember:** To calculate your personal rate of return, do not just look at the net asset value in the paper. Using the latest statement you have received from the fund company (Figure 7.1, adapted from a typical statement), fill out the form shown in Figure 7.2.

In assessing fund performance, you must also refer to the published *beta* of the funds being considered in order to determine the amount of risk involved. As discussed previously, beta is a measure of risk. It is based on the price swings of a fund compared with those of the market as a whole, measured by the Standard & Poor's 500-stock index. The higher the beta, the greater the risk.

		Dollar	Share	
Date	Transaction	Amount	Price	Shares
	Beginning balance			32.501
07/01/87	Investment	$ 50.00	$18.75	2.667
09/07/87	Investment	100.00	20.63	4.847
09/25/87	Cash dividend at 0.26	10.40	—	—
10/02/87	Investment	100.00	21.53	4.645
11/30/87	Investment	150.00	19.55	7.673
12/31/87	Cash dividend at 0.26	13.60	—	—
12/31/87	Capital gain reinvst. at 1.03	53.90	20.01	2.694
02/27/88	Investment	50.00	20.15	2.481
	Total shares			57.508

YOUR MUTUAL FUND, INC.

Figure 7.1 Information typical of a mutual fund statement.

	Example	Your Fund
1. The number of months for which your fund's performance is being measured	8	_____
2. Your investment at the beginning of the period: multiply the number of shares you owned by the NAV [(32.501 + 2.667) × $18.75]	$659.40	_____
3. The ending value of your investment: multiply the number of shares you currently own by the current NAV (57.508 × $20.15)	$1158.79	_____
4. Total dividends and capital gains received in cash ($10.40 + $13.60)	$24.00	_____
5. All additional investments (any redemptions subtracted) ($100 + $100 + $150 + $50)	$400.00	_____
6. Computation of your gain or loss		
Step (a): Add line 2 to one half of the total on line 5 [$659.4 + ½ ($400)]	$859.40	_____
Step (b): Add line 3 and line 4, then subtract one half of the total on line 5 [($1158.79 + $24) − ½ ($400)]	$982.79	_____
Step (c): Divide the Step (b) sum by the Step (a) sum ($982.79/$859.40)	1.144	_____
Step (d): Subtract the numeral 1 from the result of Step (c), then multiply by 100 [(1.144 − 1) × 100]	14.4	_____
7. Computation of your annualized return: divide the number of months on line 1 into 12; multiply the result by the percentage in Step (d) [(12/8) ×14.4]	21.6%	_____

Figure 7.2 Figuring your personal rate of return.

Beta	What it means
1.0	A fund moves up and down just as much as the market.
>1.0	The fund tends to climb higher in bull markets and dip lower in bear markets than the S&P index.
<1.0	The fund is less volatile (risky) than the market.

Betas for individual funds are widely available in many investment newsletters and directories. An example is *Value Line Investment Survey*.

Mutual Fund Ratings

You can get help in selecting mutual funds from a number of sources, including investment advisory services that charge fees. More readily available sources, however, include magazines like *Money*, *Forbes*, *Barron's* and *Personal Finance*. *Money* has a "Fund Watch" column appearing in each monthly issue. In addition, it ranks about 450 funds twice a year in terms of fund performance and risk. *Forbes* has an annual report covering each fund's performance in both up and down markets. *Value Line Investment Survey* shows the make-up of the fund's portfolio *beta* values. Information about no-load funds is contained in *The Individual Investor's Guide to No-Load Mutual Funds* (American Association of Individual Investors, 612 N. Michigan Ave., Chicago, IL 60611). **Remember:** You should not choose a fund only on the basis of its performance rating. You should consider *both performance and risk (beta)*.

How to Choose a Mutual Fund

What mutual fund to choose is not an easy question, and there is no sure answer. It will be advisable to take the following steps:

1. Develop a list of funds that appear to meet your investment goals.

2. Obtain a prospectus for each fund. In the prospectus, you will find the fund's investment objectives, risk factors, and investment limitations. **Recommendation:** Also request the Statement of Additional Information, which includes the details of fees and lists of investments; a copy of the annual report; and the most recent quarterly report.

3. Make sure the fund's investment objectives and investment policies meet your goals.

4. Analyze the fund's past performance in view of its set objectives, in both *good* markets and *bad* markets. The quarterly and annual statements issued by the fund will show results for the previous year and, probably, a comparison with the S&P 500. Look at historical performance over a 5- or 10-year period. Look for *beta* figures in investment newsletters and directories. Also, read the prospectus summary section of per-share and capital changes. **Note:** *Money, Forbes,* and other investment periodicals publish semiannual or annual performance data on mutual funds.

5. From the prospectus, try to determine some clues as to management's ability to accomplish the fund's investment objectives. Scrutinize the record, experience, and capability of the management company.

6. Note what securities comprise the fund's portfolio to see how they look to you. **Note:** Not all mutual funds are fully diversified. Not all mutual funds invest in high-quality companies.

7. Compare various fees (such as redemption, management, and sales charges, if any) and various shareholder services offered by the funds being considered (such as the right of accumulation, switch privileges within fund families, available investment plans, and a systematic withdrawal plan).

Conclusion

The basic advantages of mutual fund investments include diversification, professional management, good return, and convenience. Mutual fund shares can be purchased on a regular account or through either a voluntary or contractual savings plan. Various types of mutual funds are available. First, obtain and study a fund's prospectus to see if its investment goal matches yours. Second, select a fund which performed well in both good and bad markets. Third, choose a no-load fund. Historically, load funds have performed no better than no-loads. Know how to calculate overall return on your mutual fund investment, incorporating all three ingredients: net asset value, dividends, and capital gain distributions.

Part 3

Managing for a Lifetime of Financial Security

8

Where and How You Choose to Live

Homeownership is perhaps the most sizable investment you will ever make in your life. Further, your home is a tax shelter. There are many questions surrounding homeownership. In this chapter, you will find the answers to the following important questions:

- Should you buy or rent?
- How do you price a home?
- How much can you afford to pay for a house?
- How do you shop for an adjustable rate mortgage?
- Should you refinance your home?
- Should you pay off your mortgage early?
- How good is your homeowners' policy?
- How can you get top dollar for your house?
- How do you sell your home yourself?

Chapter 9, "How to Take on and Manage Debt," contains additional information on borrowing to buy a home.

Should You Buy a Home or Rent?

For many people, the decision to buy a home is more emotional
than economic. But if you are wondering whether or not to go on
renting, here are some questions to help you make the decision as
rationally as possible.

- Do you have enough money to put down to buy a home? The
initial cost of home ownership can be substantial. For example, for
a $100,000 house you should figure on having between $10,000 to
$20,000 (10–20 percent) for the down payment, $3000 to $6000
(3 to 6 percent) for closing costs, and a $2000 cushion for
contingencies. Thus, at the time of purchase you will need to pay
between $15,000 and $28,000 in cash.
- Are you the roving kind? If you stand a good chance of being
relocated in a few years, it doesn't make sense to incur the high
costs of borrowing, closing, and commission involved in buying a
home.
- Do you live in an area where renting makes sense? In regions
where there is a housing glut and where rent controls and values
are flat or falling, renting ends up being a bargain.
- Are you lazy, or a born renter? Can you deal with home
maintenance and lawn mowing? Or would you rather rent and
leave these tasks to a landlord? Are you enjoying the appeal of
community living and access to amenities such as swimming
pools and tennis courts?

The disadvantages of renting are primarily financial and economic. Owning a home is still the best tax shelter there is. The
renter does not receive any federal tax-deductible benefit from
rent payments. Also, rent payments do not contribute to building
your equity. You are at the mercy of rent increases and the
landlord.

Homeownership has the following advantages:

- You are building equity, due to appreciation in the value of your home.
- Interest and property taxes are deductible on your tax return.
- Owning is usually less costly than renting.
- You may enjoy extra living space and privacy.
- Single-family homes are usually in better locations than apartments.
- You will have a sense of stability and roots in the community.
- You will enjoy pride of ownership.

Note: The disadvantages of homeownership tend to be the advantages of renting, and vice versa.

In comparing rental and purchase costs, the worksheet in Figure 8.1 can be useful.

What Price to Pay

After you have found the house you like, you must decide what price to pay for it. In most cases, there is room between the price sellers ask and the price they are willing to accept. Make sure that you are not paying more for a property than its market value. To determine the maximum price to pay for the property is not an easy task. Two methods are widely used in practice.

- Have your real estate agent run "comparative-sales" on a computer. The computer should be able to give you the recent history of sales in the neighborhood. The price that a subject property can bring must be adjusted upward or downward to reflect the difference between the subject property and compar-

RENTAL COST	
Annual rental cost ($850 × 12)	$10,200
PURCHASE COSTS (assuming a 30% tax bracket)	
Add:	
Mortgage payment ($100,000 at 10%, 30 years)	10,608
Principal = $608 (approximate)	
Interest = $10,000 (approximate)	
Property taxes	1,300
Property insurance	250
Maintenance	400
Cost of lost interest on $20,000 at 5% (after-tax rate of return)	1,000
Subtract:	
Principal reduction in loan balance	(608)
Tax savings due to mortgage interest deduction ($10,000 × .3)	(3,000)
Tax savings due to property tax deduction ($1,300 × .3)	(390)
Net annual after-tax purchase costs	$9,560
Annual benefit of buying	$ 640*

* Note that the annual benefit does not include appreciation in the value of your home.

Figure 8.1 Worksheet for comparing rental and purchase costs.

ables. Since this particular approach is based on selling prices, not asking prices, it can give you a good idea about the market.

▪ Use an expert. You might want to hire a professional real estate appraiser for a fee. Appraisal is not a science but a complex and subjective procedure that requires good information about specific properties, their selling prices, and applicable terms of financing. The use of an expert may well be worth the cost if you worry about the possibility of paying too much.

How Much Can You Afford to Spend for Housing?

An accurate way to determine what kind of house you can afford is to make two basic calculations: How much can you pay each month for the long-term expenses of owning a home (e.g., mortgage payments, maintenance and operating expenses, insurance, and property taxes)? And how much cash do you have to spend for the initial costs of the purchase (e.g., the down payment, points, and closing costs)?

Many lenders use various rules of thumb to determine a borrower's housing affordability.

35-Percent Rule of Thumb.   A borrower can afford to spend no more than 35 percent of monthly take-home pay on mortgage payments.

EXAMPLE 8.1

Your gross annual income is $33,000 per year and take-home pay is $2095 per month. According to the 35-percent rule, you could afford a monthly payment of $733. Using this figure along with the mortgage rate (variable or fixed), the mortgage term, and a mortgage payment schedule, the lender can determine how much you can qualify for. For example, with an interest rate of 13 percent and a 30-year term, you could borrow $66,300. Assume that your budget has already provided for property taxes, insurance, and maintenance expenses, and you have $20,000 available for a down payment (after point charges and closing costs). You could buy a house that costs about $86,300 ($20,000 plus the $66,300 mortgage).

Multiple of Gross Earnings Rule.   The price of your home should not exceed roughly 2 to 2½ times your family's gross annual income.

EXAMPLE 8.2

If your annual gross income is $40,000, the maximum price you could afford would be $80,000 (2 times $40,000) to $100,000 (2.5 times $40,000).

Percent of Monthly Gross Income Rule.   Your monthly mortgage payment, property taxes, and insurance should not exceed 25–28 percent of your family's monthly gross income, or about 35 percent for a Federal Housing Administration (FHA) or Veterans Administration (VA) mortgage.

EXAMPLE 8.3

You and your spouse have a gross income of $60,000 ($5000 a month). Under this rule, your monthly mortgage payment, property taxes, and insurance should not exceed $1250 (25 percent of $5000) to $1400 (28 percent of $5000). That means you could qualify for a 30-year fixed-rate loan (with 10–20 percent down) at less than a 12 percent rate.

Total Debt Payments Rule.   Your debt payments on loans of 10 months or longer, including your mortgage, should not exceed 36 percent of your gross income, 50 percent for an FHA or VA loan.

EXAMPLE 8.4

You and your spouse have a gross income of $60,000 ($5000 a month). If you have a monthly debt load of $500 or less, you might look for a $120,000 house with total monthly housing payments of about $1300, since a total debt payment of $1800 ($1300 plus $500) equals or is close to 36 percent of $5000 monthly gross income. That means you could most likely qualify for a 30-year fixed-rate loan (with 10–20 percent down) even if rates hit 12 percent.

Does It Pay to Refinance Your House?

Whether refinancing is worthwhile depends on the costs of refinancing and the time required to recoup those costs through low mortgage payments. The costs of refinancing are the closing costs, which can vary widely. Closing costs include;

- Title search
- Insurance (such as hazard, title, and private mortgage insurances)
- Lender's review fees
- Buyer's loan points
- Reappraisal fees
- Credit report
- Escrow fees
- Lawyer fees
- Document preparation fees, judgment reports, notary fees, and recording fees.

To get a rough estimate of the closing costs, take the cost of refinancing (3 to 6 percent of the outstanding principal) and multiply it by the amount of the loan.

EXAMPLE 8.5

If the loan amount is $100,000 and the cost is, say, 5 percent, the closing costs are $5000.

Rule of thumb: To refinance successfully, you should plan on staying in the house for at least three years and should be able to reduce the rate paid on the mortgage by at least two percentage points.

If you are a fixed-rate mortgage holder, you might look for another fixed-rate home loan at least two to three percentage points below the mortgage currently held. If you have an adjustable loan, you might consider what the expected rate on the adjustable-rate mortgage (ARM) will be several years hence. If the current rates on fixed mortgages are substantially below the expected rate on the ARM, it might pay to refinance.

Rule of thumb: The factor to consider when refinancing is the amount of time it will take to recoup the costs of refinancing.

EXAMPLE 8.6

Assume that refinancing is $75,000. A 14 percent mortgage involves closing fees of $3750, and the new interest rate is 10 percent. At the new rate of 10 percent, the monthly payment on a 30-year fixed loan would be $658. That is a savings of $231 from the monthly payment of $889 required on a 14 percent loan. Dividing the total refinancing cost of $3750 by $231 gives a recovery period of about 16 months. Table 8.1 illustrates the monthly and yearly savings from refinancing to a 10 percent 30-year fixed-rate mortgage for $75,000.

How to Shop for an Adjustable-Rate Mortgage

With an adjustable-rate mortgage (ARM), the interest rate is not fixed but changes over the life of the loan. ARMs are often called variable or flexible rate mortgages.

Table 8.1   Savings from Refinancing

Present mortgage rate	Current monthly payment	Monthly payment at 10%	Monthly savings at 10%	Annual savings at 10%
12.0%	$771	$658	$113	$1356
12.5	800	658	142	1704
13.0	830	658	172	2064
13.5	859	658	201	2412
14.0	889	658	231	2772
15.0	948	658	290	3480

Adjustable-rate mortgages often feature attractive starting interest rates and monthly payments. But you face the risk that your payments will rise. Pluses of ARMs include:

- You pay lower initial interest (often 2 or 3 percentage points below that of a fixed rate) and lower initial payments, which can mean considerable savings. This means that ARMs are easier to qualify for.
- Payments come down if interest rates fall.
- Loans are more readily available than fixed-rate mortgages, and their processing time is quicker.
- Many adjustables are assumable by a borrower, which can help when it comes time to sell.
- Many ARMs allow you to prepay the loan without penalty.

Some of the pitfalls of ARMs include:

- Monthly payments can go up if interest rates rise.
- Negative amortization can occur. **Note:** Negative amortization happens when the monthly payments do not cover all of

the interest cost. The interest cost that is not covered is added to the unpaid principal balance. This means that after making many payments you could owe more than you did at the beginning of the loan balance.

- The initial interest rates last only until the first adjustment, typically six months or one year. And the promotional or "tease" rate is often not distinguished from the true contract rate, which is based on the index to which the loan is tied.

    Tip: It pays to get an ARM if you are buying a starter home or expect to move or be transferred in two or three years.

    You should consider a fixed-rate loan over an ARM if one or more of the following applies to you:

- You plan to be in the same home for a long time.
- You do not expect your income to rise.
- You plan to take sizable debts, like auto or educational loans.
- You prize the security of constant payments.

When you shop for an ARM (or for any other adjustable-rate loan), you should carry the following checklist of questions to ask lenders:

- What is the initial loan rate and the annual percentage rate (APR)? What costs besides interest does the APR reflect? What are the points?
- What is the monthly payment?
- What index is the loan tied to? How has the index moved in the past? Will the rate always move with the index?
- What is the lender's margin above the index?   **Tip:** The margin is an important consideration when comparing ARM loans, because it never changes during the life of the loan.   **Remember:** Index rate plus margin equals ARM interest rate.

EXAMPLE 8.7

You are comparing ARMs offered by two different lenders. Both ARMs are for 30 years and amount to $65,000. Both lenders use the one-year Treasury index, which is 10 percent. But Lender A uses a 2 percent margin, and Lender B uses a 3 percent margin. Here is how the difference in margin would affect your initial monthly payment:

	Lender A	Lender B
ARM interest rate	12% (10% + 2%)	13% (10% + 3%)
Monthly payment	$668.60 at 12%	$719.03 at 13%

- How long will the initial rate be in effect? Will there be an automatic increase at the first adjustment period, even if the index has not changed? How will this affect monthly payments?
- How often can the rate change?
- Is there a limit on each rate change, and how will the limit affect monthly payments?
- What is the "cap," or ceiling, on the rate change over the life of the loan?
- Does the loan require private mortgage insurance (PMI), and how much does it cost per month?
- Is negative amortization possible?
- Is the loan assumable?
- Is there a prepayment penalty?

Should You Pay Off Your Mortgage Early?

Suppose you have decided to refinance your home with a lower fixed-rate mortgage. You should consider the term of the loan.

Although the standard 30-year mortgage is still very much alive and well, you might want to consider the loan with a shorter term, such as a 15-year fixed rate loan. The overall savings in interest paid to the lender over the life of the 15-year mortgage can be quite substantial, yet the monthly payment is not significantly higher. **Recommendation:** Even if you decide to stay with your current 30-year mortgage, you might be able to save a bundle by paying off more each month, treating the 30-year loan as if it were a 15-year loan.

EXAMPLE 8.8

Suppose you currently have a $100,000 30-year fixed rate mortgage at 13 percent. Your monthly payment for principal and interest is $1106.20. You have decided to refinance your home with a fixed-rate loan at 10 percent. You have two options available: a 30-year loan at 10 percent, and a 15-year loan at the same rate. Look at Table 8.2 for comparisons regarding monthly payment and total interest over the life of the loan. **Note:** In

Table 8.2 Comparison of 30-Year versus 15-Year Fixed Rate Mortgage

	30-year	15-year	Increase (decrease)	Percent increase (decrease)
Principal	$100,000	$100,000	—	—
Rate	10%	10%	—	—
Monthly payment	877.57	1074.61	197.04	22.45%
Total interest	215,925	93,430	(122,495)	(56.73%)

either case, the monthly payment is less than the 13 percent mortgage. Between 30-year and 15-year, however, the monthly payment increases about 22.45 percent, while the savings in total interest payments over the life would be almost 57 percent. From this example, you learn some valuable lessons:

1. It was a good decision to refinance your home, since, in either case, you save in your monthly payments ($1106.20 vs. $877.57 or $1074.61). In this example, a 3 percent drop in the fixed rate made this possible.

2. You would be able to save $122,495 in total interest payments by election of a 15-year loan, without increasing your monthly burden.

3. Among other advantages, you will be a 100 percent equity holder in your home within 15 years instead of 30 years.

How Good Is Your Homeowner's Policy?

All homeowners policies do not offer equal protection. When a loss occurs, it is painfully easy to find out too late that a small extra premium could have saved you a large sum of money. You may also be missing out on money-saving discounts that have come along in recent years. The time to find out is *before* something happens to your home. Here are some tips:

- Determine your insurance needs. The best figure to use is the replacement value—the amount it would cost to rebuild, excluding land. Your minimum protection should be 80 percent of the cost of replacing your house.

- Distinguish the basic policy from the broad policy. Look for the broadest coverage for the dollar. But for maximum peace of mind, choose the "all risk" form. Compare the cost of each form.

- Find out if, in case of loss, you will be paid based on book value or replacement cost. You don't want the surprise of filing a claim only to learn that policies that promise "actual cash value" are actually referring to your original cost minus accumulated depreciation over years of use.

- Make sure potential calamities are covered. Fire and storm damage will always be included, but damage from ice and snow may not be.

- Look into a floater policy for furs, jewelry, silver, personal computers. Theft protection for such valuables may be limited.

- Consider an umbrella liability policy. A lawsuit over an accident on your property or away from home could wipe you out. **Note:** Umbrella protection is written over an underlying homeowners' policy and an auto policy. It takes over when the liability limits on these policies are reached.

EXAMPLE 8.9

If your homeowners' policy covers liability up to $50,000, an umbrella policy can cover you for losses in excess of $50,000.

- Achieve substantial savings by accepting a higher deductible (e.g., $250 or $500 instead of $100).

- Realize discounts by installing dead-bolt locks, smoke detectors, and fire extinguishers. See what other discounts a policy can offer you, in what ways.

- Keep pictures of your valuables and personal belongings.

- Review your insurance at least once a year, to make sure your coverage is keeping pace with inflation.

When you have to file a claim . . .

- Report any theft or vandalism to the police.
- Call your insurance agent immediately.
- Protect your property from further damage.
- Save all receipts for reimbursements.
- Make a list of damaged articles.
- Review the settlement steps outlined in your policy. In case there is a significant difference between what the insurer offers and what you believe you are entitled to, submit the dispute to arbitration. **Recommendation:** If you are unhappy with your experience with the insurance carrier (e.g., delay in receiving payment, inadequate reimbursement), "shop around" for another insurance company.

How to Get Top Dollar for Your House

Getting top dollar for your house when you sell hinges upon a number of factors. They are:

- Ask the right price. Get several brokers to look at your house. Have them do "comps" on their computer.
- Sell by July. Statistics show that of all home sales, over 70 percent occur in just four months, April through July. Most buyers want to move before school starts for their children.
- Put some cosmetics on your house. It is usually worth investing some money to put a pretty face on your house.
- Pick a top sales agent. See if you can find a "Realtor of the Year" type, because he or she is a performing broker.

- Don't be stingy on the standard commission. A full-priced broker may give up some portion of the commission to clinch your sale.

- Sign up for a shorter-term listing (e.g., no more than 90 days).

- Take advantage of a multiple listing.

- Do not oversell. Sit back and let the broker do the talking. You don't want to point out too many things (such as a fireplace) about your house.

- Avoid any offer that is contingent on the buyer's selling his or her own house. Avoid any chance the deal may fall through.

Would You Want to Sell Your Home Yourself?

Where houses are selling briskly—in places such as New England and California—"For Sale by Owner" deals are becoming popular. Although this may not necessarily be a good idea, even if it does do away with the broker's commission, here are some tips:

- *Advertise.*   Don't rely 100 percent on a "For Sale" sign on the lawn. Circulate flyers, run ads in the local newspapers and Pennysavers, and put notices on bulletin boards. Try to be creative in advertising. Highlight good points (such as an assumable mortgage and a low fixed interest rate).

- *Do not overprice.*   Compare your house to others in the neighborhood that have recently been sold, and factor in any improvements. Figure part of your savings in brokerage commissions into the asking price.

- *Screen buyers.*   Before accepting an offer, ask the buyer to fill out a financial statement. You do not want the deal to fall through because of the buyer's failure to qualify for a mortgage loan. Ask how much of a down payment can be made. A serious buyer will not resist.

- *Hire a service agency to help with the paperwork.* A service agency charges much less than a real estate agent.

Conclusion

In this chapter, various issues surrounding homeownership have been addressed. Questions that may come up at various stages of homeownership involving purchase, refinancing, maintaining, and sale of your home have been covered.

The purchase of a home is your largest single investment. Homeownership is an "American Dream." But are you really prepared to be a homeowner? Purchasing a home is a serious matter. Even after purchase, many considerations have to be taken into account. When your home goes up in value (i.e., your equity is building up) or a mortgage rate goes down, you might want to consider refinancing. Does it pay? You might want to sell your home and move to better quarters. This chapter has discussed various ways to get the most for your home, and has presented the advantages of "sale by owner."

9

How to Take On and Manage Debt

Virtually everyone uses credit every day. We live in an era of what seems to be abundant credit, which in turn allows people to spend more and more than ever before. Credit becomes a vicious cycle for many people. If you do not exercise caution, you can run into serious financial trouble, including the possibility of bankruptcy. In this chapter you will learn how to answer the following questions:

- What are the advantages and disadvantages of credit?
- How much credit can you handle?
- How do you calculate the cost of credit?
- How do you select a credit card?
- Are you managing debt properly?
- Should you pay off a loan early?
- Where can you get help for credit problems?
- Can you invest with borrowed money?
- What are the pluses and minuses of home equity lines?

How to Evaluate Credit Cards

Credit cards are an expensive way of borrowing money. Their average interest rate nationally hovers around 18 percent. But increased competition among issuers (along with the outcry of consumer groups) is pushing rates down. So it pays to comparison shop.

1. *Interest rates and annual fees.*   A simple way to compare the costs of credit cards involves two steps. First, multiply the balance you usually carry by the percentage difference between two cards you want to compare. For example, if your average annual balance is $500 and the rate difference is 5 percent, you would save $25 with the less expensive card. Second, add in the annual fees. **Do not skip this step:** A card with a lower finance charge may carry a higher annual fee. One way to save on annual fees is to reassess whether you really need as many cards as you have in your wallet, and to get rid of the cards you do not use.

2. *Grace periods.*   Do not forget the phase-out of deductibility of consumer credit interest. A 25- to 30-day period during which you can pay your bill in full and not incur an interest charge would be the next best thing to free money under the new tax law. Unfortunately, however, there is a growing trend to shorten or eliminate grace periods.

3. *Transaction fees.*   Some issuers impose a small fee each time the card is issued for a charge purchase. Many issuers also charge a fee for each cash advance, which can add up if you make frequent use of cash advances.

4. *Other fees and charges.*   These include late-payment fees and charges for exceeding your credit limit.

Rule of thumb: For most people, the best deal is a card with a low interest rate, no annual fee and a 25- to 30-day grace period. For comparison shopping, check with Bankcard Holders of America's publications, including *Women's Credit Rights, How to Shop for a Bank Card,* and *Solving Your Credit Card Billing Questions.* [Bankcard Holders of America: 333 Pennsylvania Avenue, S.E., Washington, D.C., 20003, (800) 638-6407 (outside D.C.) and (202) 543-5805.]

Warning: No matter how much your annual income may be, you should not overload yourself with too many credit cards. It can be hazardous to your credit records. They count as debts on your credit file even if they have not been used to the maximum limit.

Where to Get Credit Counseling

We are in an era when banks and stores are pressing sales pitches for credit cards and charge accounts on virtually anyone. It is not surprising that a lot of people have trouble handling the debts that go with "plastic money." Scenarios for trouble include:

- You cannot pay even the minimum amount due each month on every account.
- Your installment debts leave almost nothing for discretionary spending.
- There is no cushion for savings for an emergency.
- There is a high interest cost.

The worksheet in Figure 9.1 will give you a quick picture of your credit obligations. Be sure to list all your consumer debts, noting the maturity dates for nonrevolving charges. **Rule of thumb:** After you have totaled your monthly debt obligations, figure out the percentage of your take-home pay they represent. If the figure is higher than 15 to 20 percent, you are in danger of credit overload. Also, ask yourself if you could pay off all your debts

Name of Creditor	Interest Rate	Monthly Payment	Last Payment	Balance
	Total	_____		_____

Figure 9.1   A quick glance at your credit picture.

within 18 to 24 months. If not, you are probably "in over your head."

Painstaking Steps to Take

If, after completing the worksheet, you find you need to trim your indebtedness, try the following steps:

1. Analyze your expenses to see what you are spending, and where. Look for areas where you can cut back, at least temporarily, to free up cash and pay off debts.

2. Lock up your credit cards. Get rid of some.

3. Establish a self-imposed repayment schedule. Start with the debts that carry the highest financial charges.

4. Do not take on new debts until your present ones are under control.

Here are some tips:

1. Try to talk to creditors and rearrange a favorable repayment schedule.

2. Look for ads for debt consolidation loans at lower interest rates, with smaller monthly payments and longer repayment terms.

3. Look hard for impartial counseling from some person or organization that does not attempt to take advantage of your situation. **Recommendation:** Look for the following service: *Consumer Credit Counseling Service,* The National Foundation for Consumer Credit, 8701 George Avenue, Suite 507, Silver Spring, MD 20910. This is a nonprofit counseling service that offers counseling in areas such as budgeting, design of a debt repayment plan, and management of credit. You might look in your telephone White Pages directory for their local listings and locations.

How to Deal with a Credit Bureau

Imagine this scenario: You find yourself totally shocked when your credit application is denied. You learn that you have a bad record at the credit bureau, which you were not aware of and which is inaccurate. But you've learned this too late!!

There are about 2000 credit bureaus around the country, serving as clearinghouses for information about consumers' debts and their debt-paying habits. You do not choose a credit bureau, because it does not work for you; it works for creditors, such as banks, financial institutions, and merchants. The credit files such bureaus maintain include not only reports from creditors but public-record information about bankruptcies, lawsuits, tax liens, and other matters that could affect a consumer's creditworthiness.

Unfortunately, for whatever reason, credit bureau files may contain inaccurate information in your record. If your credit application is turned down, federal law requires that you be told why automatically. It is good to check and find out whether outdated or erroneous data was the reason.

1. Call the bureau for an appointment to review your credit file or to request that the bureau mail you a copy of your file.

2. If you find incorrect information in your file, demand that the credit bureau investigate the report. You might want to send them some supporting data. If the bureau cannot verify the accuracy of the item in dispute, it must drop the information.

3. If a bureau corrects your file, ask for a revised copy. Also, have copies sent to credit grantors who got the erroneous version.

4. Review your credit record periodically, even though you will be charged. It is worth it. **Recommendation:** Check your file each year to ensure no errors have slipped in.

How Much Debt Can You Handle?

It is not easy to determine the maximum debt an individual should have. **Rule of thumb:** Keep your monthly consumer debt payments down to around 15 percent of your total monthly net income. The absolute maximum: 20 percent. Thus, if take-home pay is $2000 for the month, only $400 (20 percent of $2000) should go toward paying off items bought on credit. **Note:** The maximum limit includes payments due on credit cards and on personal, school, and car loans—but not on mortgages, home equity loans, or rent. Those obligations can account for as much as an additional 35 percent of your total monthly expenditures. The following steps can assist you in determining your debt limit:

1. Calculate your monthly consumer debt payments.

2. Determine your monthly net income (after all taxes, Social Security, and IRA contributions).

3. To calculate the most you can afford each month, multiply your monthly income by 20, 15, or 10 percent (your personal permissible debt ratio, if you will). **Rules of thumb:** If you are single and middle-aged and net $40,000 a year, you can perhaps afford 20 percent in debt. Reduce debt to 10 percent if your income is not stable (e.g., based on commissions rather than salary). If you and your working spouse take home $50,000, you can afford 20 percent. If you have children, knock it back to 15 percent. If you are retired on a fixed income, make it 10 percent.

4. To find whether your payments are within your means, subtract (1) from (3). This figure is your safety margin. If (1) is larger than (3), however, you should start taking steps suggested previously.

EXAMPLE 9.1

You are single and middle-aged and take home $40,000 a year (or $3333 a month). You carry an average monthly consumer debt payment of $1000. According to the rule of thumb, the most you can afford each month would be $667 (20 percent of $3333). Since you are well over the limit, you should seriously consider cutting down on existing debts and avoiding additional borrowing.

Are You Managing Your Debt Properly?

Here are some tips for managing debt properly:

- Avoid borrowing from the future to meet current living expenses. Are you borrowing against future raises or bonuses to pay for daily spending? If you are living beyond your means, danger lurks ahead.

- Avoid borrowing for depreciating assets. Borrow only for appreciating assets.

- What is the interest rate on each type of debt? Keep track of who is charging a higher rate, and move to the lower cost source.

- Do not collaterize a loan with savings, because a net cost will arise. Further, in the event of an emergency, the savings may not be withdrawn. Always try to buy with cash rather than on credit.

- Avoid using a bank credit card because of the high finance charge (e.g., 18 to 20 percent). It is unwise to charge and incur an 18 percent financing cost while putting money in the bank and earning only 6 percent. You should withdraw the savings and pay off the credit card balance. Otherwise, you are losing 12 percent on your money.

- Avoid using borrowed funds to invest unless the interest rate is very low and there is a dependable investment return.

EXAMPLE 9.2

You have $100,000 in a money market account earning 8 percent. You owe $7000 on your credit cards at 20 percent interest. In this case, your net worth is declining, since the borrowing cost exceeds the return on the bank account by 12 percent. You should take $7000 out of the bank account to pay the credit cards. Otherwise, your reduction in wealth on an annual basis is:

Cost of credit card	$7000 × 20%	$1400
Return on bank account	7000 × 8%	560
Decline in wealth		$ 840

- Always pay off the high interest loans first.

- Establish a line of credit before it is necessary. There is usually no charge for a preapproved line until borrowing takes place.

- To reduce credit payments, a loan may be extended over a longer time period (e.g., financing the purchase of a car over four years rather than three years).

Advantages of Buying on Credit

- *Convenience.*   You do not have to pay by cash or give a check.

- *Safety.*   You do not need to carry lots of currency.

- *Purchasing power.*   You can buy high-ticket items and pay it out later.

- *Emergency use.*   When an unexpected expenditure occurs and you are temporarily out of cash, you can pay on credit.

- *Inflationary protection.*   You can buy goods or services before large inflationary price increases take place.

- *Ease of returning merchandise bought.*   When you have not yet paid cash for an item, returning it may be easier.

- *No charge for credit.*   If you pay within the credit billing period, you may not have to pay a finance charge.

Disadvantages of Buying on Credit

- *Over-extension.*   You may buy items you cannot afford.

- *High financing cost.*   Some credit cards involve a high fee.

- *Insecurity.*   Credit creates insecurity and anxiety on the part of many people.

How Do You Determine the Cost of Credit?

You can determine the cost of credit in two ways: (1) in terms of total dollars, and (2) in terms of an annual percentage rate (APR).

Total Dollar Cost

In terms of total dollar cost, you can immediately see your out-of-pocket expense for the use of credit. Many banks offer different mortgage programs, varying in interest rates quoted and up-front points.

EXAMPLE 9.3

You want to take out a $100,000 mortgage for a new house. Bank A has an interest rate of 8 percent and points of 2 percent. Bank B has an interest rate of 9 percent with no points required. The mortgage term is 20 years. Which bank arrangement should you go for? First, the yearly payments can be computed as follows:

(Bank A) $100,000/9.81815 = $10,185
(Bank B) $100,000/9.12855 = $10,955

The total interest and point charges for the mortgages from both banks are:

Bank A:
   Interest charge
      Total payments $10,185 × 20 $203,700
      Less: Principal   100,000 $103,700
   Points in first year $100,000 × 2%   2,000
      Total $105,700

Bank B:
Interest charge		
Total payments $10,955 × 20	$219,100	
Less: Principal	100,000	$119,100
Points in first year		0
Total		$119,100

The mortgage from Bank A should be selected because its overall cost is lower by $13,400 ($119,100 minus $105,700).

Annual Percentage Rate (APR)

Comparing different plans normally requires the use of the so-called annual percentage rate. Banks often quote their interest rates in terms of dollars of interest per hundred dollars. Other lenders quote in terms of dollars per payment. This leads to confusion on the part of borrowers. Fortunately, APR can eliminate this confusion. The APR is the simple interest rate established for the use of a given amount of money (principal) for a period of one year. The interest charge equals:

$$\text{Interest} = \text{principal} \times \text{rate} \times \text{time}$$

The APR, however, acts as a common denominator to all programs. You will be able to convert the dollar cost of credit into a single rate, i.e., APR, using the following formula:

$$\text{APR} = 2MC/[P(N + 1)]$$

where M = Number of payments of one year
C = Dollar cost of credit
P = Original proceeds from credit
N = Total number of payments in the debt contract.

EXAMPLE 9.4

Bank A offers a 7 percent car loan if you put down 25 percent of the total cost. Therefore, if you buy a $4000 auto you will finance

$3000 over a three-year period with carrying charges amounting to $630 (7 percent of $3000, for three years). You calculate that you will make equal monthly payments of $100.83 for 36 months.

Bank B will lend $3500 on the same car. You must pay $90 per month for 48 months. Which of the above quotas offers the best deal?

The APR calculations follow:

Bank A: APR = 2 × 12 × [630/3000(36 + 1)] = 13.6%
Bank B: APR = 2 × 12 × [820/3500(48 + 1)] = 11.5%

In the case of Bank B, it was necessary to multiply $90 by 48 months to arrive at a total time cost of $4320. Therefore, the total credit cost is $820 ($4320 minus $3500).

In this particular example, you should choose Bank B over Bank A. **Note:** You can choose between a larger down payment and higher monthly payments, or a smaller down payment and smaller monthly payments for a longer period of time. Without the APR, it would be difficult to determine the "best deal."

Would You Want to Borrow Money to Invest?

It should be pointed out that while low debt reduces financial burden and risk in time of economic hardship, it also reduces gain potential, since you cannot use leverage. If you are into investing, the successful use of leverage will maximize profits and net worth. Successful use of leverage results when your return on investing debt funds exceeds the cost of that debt. For example, if you borrow at 12 percent but earn 15 percent on the debt funds, your net return is 3 percent. This is earning a return while using other people's money (OPM).

Is It a Good Idea to Obtain a Home Equity Loan?

Under the Tax Reform Act of 1986, interest incurred on your first and second homes is deductible for tax purposes. However, limitations exist on the deductibility of other types of interest—especially interest on consumer loans. As a result, you should convert your consumer loan interest to interest on a home equity loan, in order to continue the full tax-deductibility of your interest expenses. The home equity loan comes in two forms: a second trust deed (mortgage) and an equity loan.

- *Second trust deed.* A second trust deed is similar to a first trust deed (mortgage), except that in the event of foreclosure, the holder of the first mortgage has priority in payment over the holder of the second mortgage.

- *Line of credit.* Under the line of credit provision, you may write a check when you need funds. You are charged with interest only on the amount borrowed.

Before you join the rush to a home equity loan, you should consider its pluses and minuses.

Advantages of a Home Equity Loan

- *Low interest rates.* This is because the loan is secured by your house, and because these loans usually bear variable rates.
- *No loan processing fees.* You do not have to go through a loan application and incur fees each time you borrow money.
- *Convenience.* You may write a check only when you need money. You are charged interest only on the amount borrowed.

Pitfalls

- *High points.*   Points imposed on an equity loan are based on the amount of the credit line, not on the amount actually borrowed.   **Warning:** Many home equity loans have no caps on interest rates.

- *Long payback period.*   It is convenient to have to pay a small minimum amount each month, but stretching out the loan payback period usually means higher interest rates over the period.

- *High balloon payments.*   Some loans require a large balloon payment of the principal at the end of the loan period.

- *Risk of home loss.*   Unlike other loans, a home equity loan involves the risk of losing your home if you cannot sell it fast enough, at a fair market price, to be able to meet the balloon requirement.

- *Frivolous spending habits.*   You may get into the habit of spending on unnecessary things.

Warning: Use home equity loans very conservatively. You may easily end up borrowing up to the limit and struggling through each month with a heavy repayment burden. **Don't forget:** Your home—and the equity it represents—is probably your biggest investment. Anything borrowed against it must be repaid upon its sale. You would lose your home if your equity line becomes greater than your ability to pay it back.

Recommendation: You should shop around and carefully compare the various equity loan alternatives in terms of each of the above pitfalls. Alternatively, you could obtain a traditional second trust deed. See Chapter 8 for additional details on borrowing and home ownership.

Should You Pay Off Your Loan Early?

Most lenders allow you to pay off a loan before its scheduled maturity without a prepayment penalty. In fact, they will refund your interest charges. The question then is: How early should you pay off your loan?   **Tip:** You should know how much interest you will save prior to a prepayment decision, because you might be better off investing the funds elsewhere rather than prepaying the loan.

You might think you save an equal amount of interest each month. Unfortunately, lenders compute interest differently. They use the Rule of 78—sometimes called the Sum of the Digits—which results in your paying more interest in the beginning of a loan, when you have the use of more of the money, and less and less interest as the debt is reduced. Therefore, it is important to know how much interest you can save by prepaying after a certain month, and how much you still owe on the loan.

EXAMPLE 9.5

You borrow $3180 ($3000 principal and $180 interest) for 12 months, so your equal monthly payment is $265 ($3180/12). You want to know how much interest you save by prepaying after six payments. You might guess $90 ($180 times 6/12), reasoning that interest is charged uniformly each month. Good guess, but wrong. Here is how the Rule of 78 works.

First, add up all the digits for the number of payments scheduled to be made, in this case the sum of the digits 1 through 12.

$$1+2+3 \ldots +12=78$$

Generally, you can find the sum of the digits (SD) using the following formula, where n equals the number of months:

$$SD = n(n+1)/2 = 12(12+1)/2 = (12)(13)/2 = 156/2 = 78$$

The sum of the digits for a four-year (48-month) loan is 1176:

$$(48)(48+1)/2 = (48)(49)/2 = 1176$$

Please refer to Figure 9.2 (loan amortization schedule). In the first month, before making any payments, you have the use of the entire amount borrowed. You thus pay 12/78 (or 15.39 percent) of the total interest in the first month. In the second month, you pay 11/78 (14.10 percent); in the third, 10/78 (12.82 percent); and so on down to the last payment, 1/78 (1.28 percent). Thus, the first month's total payment of $265 contains $27.69 (15.39 percent of $180) in interest and $237.31 ($265 minus $27.69) in principal. The twelfth and last payment of $265 contains $2.30 (1.28 percent of $180) in interest and $262.70 in principal.

In order to find out how much interest is saved by prepaying after the sixth payment, you merely add up the digits for the remaining six payments. Thus, using the above formula:

$$6(6+1)/2 = 21$$

This means that 21/78 of the interest, or $48.46 (21/78 times $180), will be saved.

To calculate the amount of principal still owed, subtract the total amount of interest already paid, $131.54 ($180−$48.46), from the total amount of payments made, $1590 (6 × $265), giving $1458.46. Then subtract this from the original $3000 principal, giving $1541.54 still owed.

Does it pay to pay off after the sixth payment? It depends on how much return you can get from investing elsewhere. In this example, you needed $1541.54 to pay off the loan to save $48.46 in interest.

Note: For loans of longer maturities, the same rules apply, though the actual sum of the digits will be different. Thus, for a 48-month loan, you would pay, in the first month, 48/1176 of the total interest; in the second month, 47/1176; and so on.

Payment Number	Fraction (Percent) Earned by Lender	Monthly Payment	Interest	Principal
	Based on a loan of $3180 ($3000 principal and $180 interest)			
1	12/78 (15.39%)	$265	$27.69*	$237.31**
2	11/78 (14.10%)	265	25.39	239.61
3	10/78 (12.82%)	265	23.08	241.92
4	9/78 (11.54%)	265	20.77	244.23
5	8/78 (10.26%)	265	18.46	246.54
6	7/78 (8.97%)	265	16.15	248.85
7	6/78 (7.69%)	265	13.85	251.15
8	5/78 (6.41%)	265	11.54	253.46
9	4/78 (5.13%)	265	9.23	255.77
10	3/78 (3.85%)	265	6.92	258.08
11	2/78 (2.56%)	265	4.62	260.38
12	1/78 (1.28%)	265	2.30	262.70
78	78/78 (100%)	$3180	$180.00	$3000.00

*$27.69 = $180.00 × 12/78 (15.39%).
** $237.31 = $265 − $27.69.

Figure 9.2 Loan amortization schedule.

For more information on early payoff of a mortgage loan, see Chapter 8.

Financing an Automobile

Primary Considerations

What should you consider in financing a car?   **Recommendation:** You may be able to get a better deal on a car loan from another source (e.g., credit union, bank) than you can from the auto dealer. Consider the provisions in the loan agreement regarding prepayment of the loan. Will there be a complete forgiveness of future finance charges if you can repay the loan in advance? What is the interest penalty for late payments? What rights do you have in the event of repossession? Is there an acceleration clause stating that all payments are due immediately if one payment is not made on time?

Above all, be sure you can meet the monthly payments if you buy your auto on credit. The monthly payments should not be more than one-half of your monthly housing costs.

EXAMPLE 9.6

You buy a car for $14,000, making a down payment of $3000. You will finance the balance at an interest rate of 24 percent, payable monthly over three years.

Cost of auto	$14,000
Less: down payment	3,000
To be financed	$11,000

Monthly interest rate = 24%/12 = 2%
Months 3 × 12 = 36

According to Table 2.4, "Present Value of Annuity of $1," when $i=2\%$ and $n=36$ the factor is 25.48884.

The monthly loan payment is:

$$\frac{\$11,000}{25.48884} = \$431.56$$

Total loan payments $431.56 × 36	$15,536.16
Principal	11,000.00
Total interest	$ 4,536.16

Table 9.1 shows what the monthly finance charge will be on a $1000 loan for a 12-month, 24-month, and 36-month period.

Should You Select a Rebate or Lower Finance Charge?

To clear inventories, auto manufacturers (e.g., General Motors) may offer you an incentive to buy a car, in the form of a rebate or lower interest cost. Which is financially more attractive? Typically, the lower financing cost should be selected.

EXAMPLE 9.7

General Motors is offering an $18,000 car at either a rebate of $750 or financing at 1.9 percent. If the financing alternative is

Table 9.1 Finance Charge for Each $1000 Loan

Interest	12 months	24 months	36 months
9%	$49.42	$96.43	$144.79
10	54.99	107.48	161.62
11	60.58	118.59	178.59
12	66.19	129.76	195.72
14	77.45	152.31	230.39
16	88.77	175.11	265.65
18	100.16	198.18	301.49

taken, a down payment of 10 percent is required. The financial period is one year, with monthly payments. You can earn 8 percent on your money. Computations follow:

Savings from rebate		$750
Savings from low finance charge		
Amount subject to financing	$16,200	
Net interest earned (8.0% − 1.9%)	×6.1%	$988
Net advantage with financing the car		$238

Let the Buyer Beware: The dealer may be deceiving you in implying that something of real value is being offered. When cars have been held in inventory for some time, they are often sold at a lower price, to make room. The dealer may be discounting the car $800 anyway. But because of the promotion incentive, the price of the car is usually not discounted the typical amount. In effect, you may be saving only $188 ($988 minus $800).

If you know how to manage and control debt, you can, in effect, increase your return through the use of leverage. Balance the advantages and disadvantages of credit in deciding whether or not to use it. Take steps to keep a credit record. If a credit problem arises, try to work it out with the lender first. And then try to seek the assistance of a credit counselor.

Conclusion

People have different attitudes toward credit. Some people think credit is "good"; others say credit is "bad." But one thing is clear. Too much credit is bad. Too much debt may lead to personal disaster and bankruptcy. It's essential to manage credit wisely and judiciously: you want to obtain just the amount of credit for your needs, and to shop around to get the "best deal" on a credit card.

10

Planning for Your Children's College Education

This chapter deals with providing for your children's college education. It discusses how to save to meet future educational costs; what types and amounts of costs will be incurred; and how to make the future value calculations necessary to determine annual savings, interest rate required on funds, etc. Various sources of financial aid are identified. Information on career opportunities is also provided.

Saving for Your Child's College Education

Gifts are a simple way to build a college fund for your child while saving on income taxes. **Recommendation:** Obtain a Social Security number for your child and start an account under the Uniform Gifts to Minors Act. Encourage relatives to give gifts to the child's college fund. The gifts earn interest taxed to the child, whose tax bracket is usually much lower than the parents. Under the present tax law, a child under 14 pays tax at the child's tax rate on the first $1000 of interest or dividend income from gift money. Any interest or dividend income in excess of $1000 is taxed at the parent's tax rate. However, after the age of 14 the child's tax rate is used on all of his or her income.

EXAMPLE 10.1

A child earns interest and dividend income of $3600 on gift moneys. The parent's tax bracket is 28 percent. The tax to be paid is:

First $1000 of income taxed at child's rate	$ 0
Balance of $2600 of income taxed at parent's rate	
$2600 × .28	728
Tax	$728

You can put money away for your child's education by purchasing a zero-coupon bond, preferably with a distant maturity date. As previously discussed, interest is not taxed until the bond matures.

Another way to finance your child's education is by taking out a home equity loan, either for the principal home or the second home. **Note:** Interest is deductible on a mortgage to finance the child's education.

You can buy your child shares in a growth mutual fund, automatically reinvesting the dividends and capital gain distributions. The dividends and distributions do not amount to much; most of the money is earned from the growth in the value of the shares. Therefore, the annual yield might not exceed the $1000 limit. However, 10 years down the line there should be a significant increase in the share value. If the shares are sold after the child's fourteenth birthday, the capital gain is taxed at the child's low tax bracket.

If you have a business, you can hire your children. Their wages, if reasonable, are tax-deductible.   **Tip:** Place the money in an account for the child's future education. Further, if you have an unincorporated business, you do not have to pay Social Security tax on wages paid to children.

In 1988, your child can earn wages of $3000 without having to pay any tax. $3000 is the new standard deduction.

What Does It Cost and How Much Will You Need?

The cost of higher education has increased significantly. In fact, college costs are expected to more than double within the next 10 years. Financing the college education of your children requires you to begin saving or investing for their education well in advance. College-related costs include tuition, room, and board. At some of the most prestigious colleges, the cost per year can be about $17,000. Costs vary, depending on whether a state school or private university is chosen. The private alternative is more costly. Costs also vary among state schools, as well as among private schools. The range is significant. A four-year education at private school may cost anywhere between $20,000 to $80,000, depending on the academic standing of the institution. Costs also depend on commutation distance, living costs in the school's city, and the fees charged by the college.

Financial planning to meet college costs includes:

- Use of long-term savings plans
- Shifting income to your lower tax-bracket child
- Use of financial assistance programs

According to *The New York Times* (August 8, 1987), college tuition over the last seven years has risen faster than the inflation rate. Thus, in considering future costs, you must take into account inflationary increases. Tuition has increased at a yearly average of 8 percent at four-year private schools and 6 percent at four-year public institutions. Thus, you can extrapolate the future cost of an education at a private college by taking the current cost and factoring in a growth rate of 8 percent.

EXAMPLE 10.2

Your child wants to go to college for the next four years. The annual cost is $4500, and will increase at the rate of 8 percent per year. The cost of education is:

$4500 × future value factor (see Table 2.2, "Future Value of Annuity of $1," where *i*=8%)
$4500 × 4.50611 = $20,278

As per *The New York Times* (8/8/87), the estimated "fixed charges" at private four-year schools amount to $10,493; these include tuition, fees, and room and board. At four-year public institutions, costs will average $4104 for students living in the state. Fixed charges at private two-year institutions will rise by 6 percent to $6945 but will reach $8305 for resident students and $6737 for commuters. At public two-year colleges the average costs will increase 5 percent to $3687, but the total annual costs will reach about $3889 for commuters.

The following list of the most expensive private and public colleges is based on the College Board's Survey of the 10 costliest private and public institutions.

Private Institution	*Total Cost*
Bennington College	$17,990
Sarah Lawrence	17,440

Barnard College	17,296
University of Chicago	17,190
Columbia University	17,120

Public Institution	*Total Cost*
Colorado School of Mines	$6,724
Virginia Military Institute	6,690
University of California, San Diego	6,464
University of Rhode Island	6,027
University of Illinois, Chicago	5,934

According to the National Center for Education Statistics, a typical private college that presently costs $9020 a year will probably cost $12,075 five years from now, and $16,160 ten years from now. A typical public university that now costs about $4880 a year is anticipated to cost $6530 in five years and $8740 in ten years. Those figures include tuition, fees, books, supplies, room and board, personal expenses, and transportation. This particular source estimates the annual increase in education costs at 6 percent per year.

Education costs at private and public colleges at the four-year and two-year levels are available in the form of a publication entitled *Student Expenses at Post-Secondary Institutions.* You can obtain a copy by writing to The College Board, P.O. Box 2815, Princeton, N.J. 08541. Also available is the *College Cost Book,* published by the College Entrance Examination Board.

What about setting up an education fund for your children? The amount in the fund depends on the number of children, their ages and educational plans, scholarships and student loans available, and the amount of family income.

Estimate the total college cost for the first year. Be careful not to underestimate your costs. You want a well-prepared figure. To take into account inflation and other increased price factors, add

7 percent to the first year's cost for the second year, 15 percent for the third year, and 23 percent for the fourth year.

EXAMPLE 10.3

Your child's estimated expenses at ABC College in the first year are $6000. The projected costs for the remaining years are:

Year 2	$6000 × 1.07	$6420
Year 3	6000 × 1.15	6900
Year 4	6000 × 1.23	7380

Tip: Obtain and use a worksheet included in *Meeting College Costs* to estimate educational costs. It is a free booklet published by the College Scholarship Service.

Why not prepare a budget for your child's estimated costs at various colleges being considered? The budget may take the following form:

Tuition

Fees (admission, library, activity)

Room and board

Books and supplies

Travel to and from school

Organizational dues (e.g., fraternity)

Health costs

Clothing

Entertainment and recreation

Total budgeted cost

You can reduce costs in college in the following ways.

- Try to obtain credit by examination; this lowers the number of credits you have to pay for while in school.
- See if the college will offer special payment plans.
- If possible, make use of a cooperative education program.
- Pick a low-cost college. This list shows college types in ascending order from less costly to more costly:
  - Public two-year college
  - State college in your own state
  - State college out of your home state
  - Private two-year college
  - Private four-year college
- Attend a three-year degree program, thus reducing tuition fees and living costs.
- Undertake an "external degree program."
- Take a college-level course in high school, and perhaps you will earn college credit for it.

Determining Need? Future Value Calculations Can Help

How much money will you need to have accumulated when your child is ready for college?

EXAMPLE 10.4

Your income is $54,000. You expect to save 12 percent of your income each year for the college education of your child, which amounts to $6480 ($54,000 times 12 percent). Therefore, each month you have to save $540 ($6480/12). You expect to earn 8 percent on your savings. Your child will be going to college 10 years from now. The future value factor (See Table 2.2, "Future Value of Annunity of $1") for $n=10$, $i=8\%$ is 14.48656. After 10 years you will have accumulated $93,873 for your child's education, as computed below:

$6480 \times 14.48656 = \$93,873$

The annual deposits in a bank account necessary to provide for your child's education may have to be computed.

EXAMPLE 10.5

You want to send your child to college 10 years from now and will need $40,000 at that time. Assuming an 8 percent interest rate, you will have to make annual deposits of $2761.18, as computed below [future value factor (see Table 2.2) for $n=10$, $i=8\%$ is 14.48656].

$$\frac{\$40,000}{14.48656} = \$2,761.18$$

You may have to determine the monthly savings required to have sufficient funds for your child's education.

EXAMPLE 10.6

In today's dollars, you will need $30,000 to provide for a college education for your child. Your child will be going to college 10 years from now. You anticipate earning a net rate of return (after considering the inflation rate) of 8 percent. At present, you have $5000 saved for your child's education.

The growth factor for $n=10$, $i=8\%$ from Table 2.1, "Future Value of $1," is 2.15892.

Your $5000 of savings will be worth $10,795 10 years from now, computed as follows:

$5000 × 2.15892 = $10,795

The additional savings needed is:

$30,000 − $10,795 = $19,205

The savings factor for $n=10$, $i=8\%$ (see Table 2.1, "Future Value of Annuity of $1") is 14.48656.

The annual savings required each year to accomplish your goal is:

$$\frac{\$19,205}{14.48656} = \$1326$$

The monthly savings is:

$$\frac{\$1326}{12} = \$111$$

You may need to know the interest rate that has to be earned on your money to have adequate funds available for your child's education.

EXAMPLE 10.7

You want to have $28,000 saved in 12 years when your child will be ready for college. The annual rate of return you must earn on your money if you invest $1500 annually is about 8 percent as computed below:

$$\frac{\$28,000}{\$1500} = 18.6667 \text{ factor}$$

According to Table 2.2, "Future Value of Annuity of $1," the interest rate for $n=12$ and a factor of 18.6667 is about 8 percent (18.97713 exactly).

You may be unsure whether it pays financially to go for a graduate degree. Present value analysis will be helpful.

EXAMPLE 10.8

The graduate degree you are considering will take you two years. The initial application fee is $100. The cost of tuition and books will be $4000 in the first year and $4800 in the second year. The salary at your job will be the same while you are in school. However, after you receive the degree your salary will be $5000, $7000, and $12,000 more in years 3, 4, and 5. If you did not go to graduate school, you could earn an extra $3000 and $4500 in years 1 and 2. Your discount rate is 10 percent. You should go for the graduate degree, as indicated below.

Table 2.3, "Present Value of $1," is used to obtain the appropriate factors (see Figure 10.1).

	Net Present Value	Year 0	Year 1	Year 2	Year 3	Year 4	Year 5
MBA		$ −100 × 1	$− 4000 ×.90909	$− 4800 ×.82645	$+ 5000 ×.75132	$+ 7000 ×.68301	$+ 12000 ×.62092
	$8286	$ −100	$− 3636	$− 3967	$+ 3757	$+ 4781	$+ 7451
No MBA			$ + 3000 ×.90909	$ + 4500 ×.82645			
	$6446		$ + 2727	$ + 3719			

Figure 10.1 Schedule of present value.

The net present value is higher with the graduate degree than without it.

Although the graduate degree will benefit you for more than five years, we cut off our analysis at five years to avoid making too many calculations which do not add further to our knowledge.

Of course, money is not the only reason to go for a graduate degree. Other motivating factors include promotion, personal satisfaction, mobility, and interest in particular subjects. **Special Note:** Seriously consider a company that will pay for your graduate education.

Sources of Financial Aid

It is important to know the fund sources available for financial aid.

- Check out federal and state government programs first, since they represent the most funding available. **Note:** You can use one form to apply for various federal, state, and college programs.

- Consider specialized programs directed toward certain types of people (e.g., based on race or religion).

- Most financial aid can be gotten by filing appropriate forms with the colleges.

- Find out about funds available from the college itself.

To find assistance for sources of financial aid for college costs, you may contact: Scholarship Search, 1775 Broadway, New York, N.Y. 10019. Scholarship Search will provide, for a fee, a computer printout of sources of scholarships, based on the applicant's background. For information on available scholarships and student college aid you may contact Student College Aid, 3641 Deal Street, Houston, Texas 77025.

A publication discussing college aid offerings is *Don't Miss Out: The Ambitious Student's Guide to Financial Aid,* published by Octameron Associates, P.O. Box 3437, Alexandria, Virginia 22302.

Financial aid information can be gotten from the high school financial aid officer, who is equipped to handle questions and also has the proper forms. Financial aid officers at the college your child is considering should also be contacted.

The Early Financial Aid Planning Service provides a computerized estimate of your eligibility for financial aid from various sources, in addition to a comprehensive analysis of your family's financial status relative to college costs and potential aid. There is a matching of available sources with your eligibility background. Information can be obtained from: Early Financial Aid Planning, Box 2843, Princeton, N.J. 08541. However, this service is not available for parents of high school seniors.

Literally hundreds of scholarships, grants, and loan programs exist to meet educational costs. Different requirements, application procedures, and amounts are available. Your child's aid program may consist of a combination of grants and loans. Compare awards received from different schools to select the one that is best for you.   **Warning:** To obtain financial aid, your child must be attending an *accredited* college.

Scholarships and grants do *not* have to be repaid. However, they are taxable to the degree they exceed tuition and course fees.

Eligibility for scholarships may be based on merit (academic or athletic) or financial need. Some other bases for scholarships are:

- Religion
- Nationality
- Race
- Occupation

Don't forget private scholarship sponsors:

- Your company
- Labor union you belong to
- Trade association your company belongs to
- Professional associations
- Advocacy groups for minorities or women
- National Merit Scholarship Corporation, for students who earn a high grade on an NMSC examination
- Civic and fraternal organization (e.g., American Legion)
- State Department of Vocational Rehabilitation, for handicapped students
- ROTC, for students who will pursue careers in the military as officers
- Other sponsors (e.g., Boy Scouts)

Information on opportunities for minorities and women can be obtained from the *Selected List of Post-Secondary Education Opportunities for Minorities and Women,* available from the Department of Health, Education and Welfare, Office of Education, Regional Office Building 3, Room 4082, Washington, D.C. 20202.

Social Security benefits may be available for unmarried full-time students who are children of disabled or retired individuals. Inquiry may be made at the Social Security office. Veteran's educational benefits may be available to veterans and their wives, widows, and children.

The amount of financial aid you will require equals the difference between college costs and the amount you can afford.

EXAMPLE 10.9

The cost for your child's education is estimated at:

Tuition and fees	$25,000	
Room and board	20,000	
Books and supplies	2,500	
Travel expenses	1,800	
Personal expenses	500	
Total cost		$49,800
Less: Amount you can afford to pay		15,000
Amount of financial aid required		$34,800

Estimating the Financial Aid Required

- Determine all costs associated with the education at the particular school, including tuition and fees, room and board, books, and travel expenses.

- Determine your share of the educational costs.

- Amount of financial aid needed equals:

      Total education costs − your share of total costs

Typically, you are eligible for financial aid equal to the amount you need.

What is financial aid? Financial need is the difference between the cost of attending college and the amount the parents and student are capable of contributing. Financial aid officials expect parents to use 5 percent of their assets each year and all their "available income" to provide for the child's education.

Available income equals:

      Taxable and nontaxable income − basic expenses (e.g., housing, food, clothing)

To get financial aid, you have to prove that you need the money. You have to show that you cannot pay the total costs on your own. It is a mistake to think that financial aid is just for poor people.

Your ability to obtain financial aid increases with the colleges that charge higher fees. Thus, if you are required to pay $2000 toward total costs, do not be concerned with whether the price tag is $6000 or $10,000, since with financial aid your net cost in either case will be $2000.

A possible way of financing your child's education is taking out a home equity loan for which the interest is fully tax-deductible. (In contrast, with a regular loan you can only deduct 20 percent of the interest in 1989, 10 percent in 1990, and none in 1991.)

Many middle-income families do not qualify for Guaranteed Student Loans and other assistance programs. For these families, regular loans may be the answer.

Available regular loans for college from the least to the most expensive include:

- A college loan with low interest, repayable after graduation
- A low-interest loan through a civic organization
- A deferred-tuition plan, if offered by the college
- A loan from a credit union
- A bank loan
- A finance company loan

Some colleges offer their own long-term loans. Usually, they are at low interest and have convenient repayment schedules.

You will have to contribute some aid toward your child's education, since financial aid sponsors require some participation on your part. Try to have your children contribute some of their savings (e.g., summer earnings) toward college education.

The amount you have to contribute toward a college education depends on a "need analysis" conducted by a national organization, for example the College Scholarship Service (CSS) of the College Board. The confidential Financial Aid Form requires you to indicate your income, expenses, assets (home equity, stock owned), obligations, and number of children (including those now in college).   **Tip:** Note unusual costs, such as those incurred by a handicapped child. The results of the "need analysis" are sent to the financial aid directors of the various colleges.

From your total assets, an asset protection allowance will be subtracted (e.g., $10,000 to $40,000) depending on your circumstances (e.g., age). Only 12 percent of the balance is considered in computing your ability to meet college costs.

EXAMPLE 10.10

Your total assets are $150,000. The asset protection allowance is $20,000. The remaining assets figure considered in deriving ability to pay for college is computed below:

Total assets	$150,000
Less: asset protection plan	20,000
	$130,000
	× 12%
Remaining assets	$ 15,600

"Needs analysis" for college aid determines your eligible assets.   **Tip:** Try to lower your eligible assets so as to obtain more college aid. Since the asset formula does not consider retirement accounts—IRAs, 401(k)s, and Keoghs—put more of your money into those accounts.

The asset formula does not deduct consumer debt from total

assets, but it does count mortgage debt. Therefore, obtain funds from a home equity loan to pay off your other debts.

Business assets do not count as much as personal assets in the aid formula. Thus, try to shift some personal assets to business assets.

To determine your ability to pay for the college education of your children, the assets figure is divided by the number of children.

If your family is richer in assets than income, you can figure the ability to pay with a different formula, based on income only. If you use that formula, you have to renounce all forms of federal aid except Guaranteed Student Loans.

Federal Government Programs

The federal government has several programs for helping families defray the costs of college education:

• *Basic Educational Opportunity Grants (BEOG)*. This program has the most funds of all federal programs. Eligibility depends on a family's financial condition. Full-time and part-time students are eligible. The grants can be used for four-year and two-year public and private colleges as well as for vocational and technical schools. To obtain information, write to P.O. Box 84, Washington, D.C. 20004.

• *Supplemental Educational Opportunity Grant (SEOG)*. The grant cannot be greater than 50 percent of the total cost of college, or 50 percent of the total aid provided. Colleges match the SEOG amount with grants from their own funds, loans, or jobs.

• *College Work-Study Program*. Part-time and summer jobs are subsidized by the federal government for students in need. In some cases, the jobs are career-related. The government will pay up to 80 percent of the salaries. Information can be obtained from the college placement office.

- *National Direct Student Loans (NDSL).* These loans are made by the college, but 90 percent of the money comes from the federal government. Eligibility and loan amount are determined by financial aid directors. Half-time students are also eligible to apply. Repayment of principal and interest (at a very low rate) does not start until nine months after studies end. All or a portion of the loan may be canceled if the graduate enters specified fields or the armed forces.

- *Guaranteed Student Loan Program (GSLP).* These loans are available without an income ceiling. Full-time or part-time students may receive loans through financial institutions (e.g., banks). The interest rate is low and repayment commences nine to twelve months after leaving college. Students at business, trade, vocational, and technical schools are also eligible. Guaranteed student loans have the following limits:

Freshmen and sophomores	$2625
Juniors and seniors	4000
Graduate students	7500

In total, an undergraduate can borrow up to $17,250. A graduate student can borrow up to a total of $54,750 for undergraduate and graduate work.

You can also apply to the state for aid. The State Student Incentive Grant Program (SSIG) involves federal government matching funds for state grants to students. Eligibility, funding, application requirements, etc. vary, depending upon the state.

An interest-sensitive life insurance policy on the life of the parent may aid in education funding. Single premium life, universal life, and other interest-sensitive insurance policies sometimes allow the withdrawal of cash from the policies, instead of a loan. If the policy is taken out when the child is young, each withdrawal could be taken later to fund his or her education. Cash up to the amount paid into the policy can be withdrawn tax-free.

What Are the Career Opportunities for Your Children?

Occupational Outlook for College Graduates, published by the Bureau of Labor Statistics, contains supply and demand information for various careers, as well as job descriptions. Another source of information on jobs is the *College Placement Annual,* which is in most libraries. Abilities tests and skills tests can be taken to determine your child's aptitude for a particular career. Most academic institutions have career planning centers where tests are administered.

Conclusion

Several means of providing for and evaluating the cost of your child's education have been presented. Computations were given on savings and costs to be incurred. Numerous available sources of financial aid were also cited.

11

How to Have Enough Money in Your Pension Plan When You Retire

Many people do not prepare for retirement, even though it is a major event in their lives. Are you adequately planning for *your* retirement? A financial advisor such as a financial planner, a CPA, or a life insurance agent may be called upon to advise you on the type of retirement plan necessary to meet your particular needs. However, you can do much financial planning for retirement yourself. You can compute the contributions necessary to achieve your retirement goal and the amounts to be received upon retirement. This chapter discusses:

- What retirement planning involves
- How to estimate retirement needs
- How to evaluate types of pension and retirement plans
- How to check your pension fund
- How to put your retirement plan to work
- How to buy annuities

What Does Retirement Planning Involve?

The first step in retirement planning is to develop retirement goals. Once these have been set, you should develop specific savings plans aimed at achieving them. You must take into account an explicit consideration of present versus future needs, and an examination of how present resources may be allocated to serve future needs.   **Note:** Your financial situation at retirement hinges not only on your plans for retirement but also on your choice of career and lifestyle.

It is essential for economic security in old age to devote some income toward retirement goals. Means of saving for retirement are Social Security, employer retirement and pension plans, annuities, and individual retirement and savings plans.   **Tip:** An easy way to plan for retirement is to state your retirement income objectives as a percent of your present earnings. For example, if you desire a retirement income of 70 percent of your final take-home pay, you and your life insurance agent or financial planner can determine the amount necessary to fund this need.

How to Estimate Retirement Needs

Retirement planning basically involves two steps: first target your retirement needs, and then estimate the annual savings necessary to meet that target. Figure 11.1 can be of help for this purpose.

A life expectancy table is given in Table 11.1. It may be difficult to determine accurately your future Social Security benefits, since these benefits are based on your highest 26 years of earnings. A helpful general rule is: The higher the income level, the more supplemental income needed to bridge the gap between current

		Sample	
1.	Current salary	$ 50,000	_____
2.	Percentage of current salary to be replaced	× .70	_____
3.	Retirement income target	$ 35,000	_____
4.	Minus: Vested defined benefits	($ 5,000)	_____
5.	Minus: Social Security benefits (assume 20% of current salary approximated from Table 11.2)	($ 10,000)	_____
6.	Required annual income from invested fund	$ 20,000	_____
7.	Life expectancy (from Table 11.1)	× 18.9	_____
8.	Required target investment	$378,000	_____

9. Present target resources:

IRA	$20,000		_____
Keogh	0		_____
Defined contribution plan	45,000		_____
Other investments	90,000		_____
Total		($155,000)	_____

10.	Required additional to target fund	$223,000	_____

Figure 11.1 Worksheet for retirement planning.

(continued)

| 11. Years to retirement | Divided by 25 | |
| 12. Current annual savings required to achieve target | $ 8,920 | |

Figure 11.1 (*continued*)

earnings and Social Security payouts. Social Security benefits to be considered are indicated in Table 11.2.

Defined Benefit Plans versus Defined Contribution Plans

All pension plans can be classified as defined benefit plans, defined contribution plans, or some combination of the two.

• *Defined benefit plan.* A defined benefit plan specifies your monthly benefit upon retirement. Each year, your employer contributes to a pension plan an amount necessary to pay for those future predetermined benefits. The amount of present contribution is based upon assumed investment returns and probabilities of survival. **Note:** With this plan, you know how much you will receive, but you do not know how much those monies will be worth. Inflation can be a discouraging factor.

• *Defined contribution plan.* Under this plan, you are not guaranteed a specified benefit at retirement. Your benefits will hinge on future contributions and the investment performance of your retirement plan. **Note:** Many defined contribution plans permit you to make an additional voluntary contribution to your retirement account.

Table 11.1 Life Expectancy by Race, Age, and Sex*

Age	Total	White Male	White Female	Black Male	Black Female
50	28.3	25.6	31.3	22.2	28.0
51	27.5	24.8	30.4	21.5	27.2
52	26.7	24.0	29.6	20.8	26.5
53	25.8	23.2	28.7	20.2	25.7
54	25.0	22.4	27.8	19.5	24.9
55	24.2	21.6	27.0	18.9	24.1
56	23.4	20.8	26.1	18.2	23.4
57	22.6	20.1	25.3	17.6	22.7
58	21.9	19.3	24.4	17.0	21.9
59	21.1	18.6	23.6	16.5	21.2
60	20.4	17.9	22.8	15.9	20.5
61	19.6	17.2	22.0	15.3	19.8
62	18.9	16.5	21.2	14.8	19.2
63	18.2	15.8	20.4	14.3	18.5
64	17.5	15.2	19.6	13.8	17.9
65	16.8	14.5	18.9	13.3	17.2
70	13.7	11.6	15.3	10.9	14.1
75	10.8	9.1	12.0	8.8	11.3
80	8.3	7.0	9.0	6.7	8.6
85 and over	6.3	5.3	6.7	4.8	6.5

* Expectation of life in years.

SOURCE: Adapted from *Statistical Abstract of the US 1986*, Table No. 108, p. 69 (United States Department of Commerce, Bureau of the Census).

Types of Pension and Retirement Plans

Two major sources of retirement income are company-sponsored pension plans and individual retirement plans.

Table 11.2 Social Security Benefits

Annual earnings	Annual Social Security amount (avg.)	Percentage of earnings replaced
$44,000 or more	$9,468	22% or less
33,000	9,144	28
24,000	8,496	35
17,000	6,672	39
12,000	5,304	44

Company-Sponsored Pension Plans

Qualified Company Retirement Plans. The IRS permits a corporate employer to make contributions to a qualified retirement plan. *Qualified* means that it meets a number of specific criteria in order to deduct contributions to the plan from taxable income. The investment income of the plan is allowed to accumulate untaxed.

Profit-Sharing Plans. A profit-sharing plan is a type of defined contribution plan. Unlike with other qualified plans, you may not have to wait until retirement to receive distributions. **Note:** Since the company must contribute only when it earns a profit, the amount of benefit at retirement is highly uncertain.

401(k) Salary Reduction Plans. In addition to, or in place of, a qualified pension plan or profit sharing plan, you may set up a 401(k) salary reduction plan, which defers a portion of your salary for retirement. This is like building a nest egg for the future by taking a *cut* in pay. Tax savings more than offset a pay cut (on paper) since you end up with more take-home pay and more retirement income.

EXAMPLE 11.1

You save 10 percent of your $40,000-a-year salary in a 401(k) plan. You are married with two children, are the only wage-earner in the family, and do not itemize deductions. See how you fare with a 401(k) plan and without one.

	Take-home pay	
	With 401(k) plan	Without 401(k) plan
Base pay	$40,000	$40,000
Salary reduction	4,000	None
Taxable income	$36,000	$40,000
Federal and FICA taxes	8,159	9,279
Savings after taxes	None	4,000
Take-home pay	$27,841	$26,721
Extra take-home pay under 401(k)	$1,120	

Note: Your retirement income will grow faster inside a tax-sheltered plan, such as 401(k), than outside one. This is because the interest you are earning will go untaxed and therefore keep compounding.

Tax-Sheltered Annuities (TSA). If you are an employee of a nonprofit institution, you are eligible for a TSA. A TSA is similar to the 401(k), but you may withdraw the funds at any age for any reason without tax penalty. **Note:** You must pay ordinary taxes on all withdrawals.

Employee Stock Ownership Plans (ESOP). ESOP is a stock-bonus plan. The contributions made by the employer are tax-deductible.

Simplified Employee Pension (SEP).   SEP is a plan whereby an employer makes annual contributions on the employee's behalf to an individual retirement account set up by the employee.

Individual Retirement Plans

If you do not have a company retirement plan, or you would like to supplement a company plan through additional private savings, the benefits of tax deferral can also be attained through individual-oriented investments, such as IRAs, Keoghs, and annuities.

What Are Individual Retirement Accounts (IRAs)?   IRAs are set up by individuals themselves. The IRA is a qualified individual retirement plan whereby your contributions not only grow tax-free but also are either tax-deductible or not included in your income. **Remember:** Under the Tax Reform Act of 1986, however, a person who is covered by an employer's retirement plan, or who files a joint return with a spouse who is covered by such a plan, may be entitled only to a partial deduction or no deduction at all, depending on adjusted gross income (AGI). The deduction begins to decrease when the taxpayer's income rises above a certain level and is eliminated altogether when it reaches a higher level. **Note:** The deduction is reduced or eliminated entirely depending on your filing status and income, as follows:

If filing status is:	Deduction is reduced if AGI is within range of:	Deduction is eliminated if AGI is:
Single, or head of household	$25,000–$35,000	$35,000 or more

| Married—joint return or qualifying widow(er) | $40,000–$50,000 | $50,000 or more |
| Married—separate return | $ 0—$10,000 | $10,000 or more |

If you are *not* covered by an employee retirement plan, you can still take a full IRA deduction of up to $2000 or 100 percent of compensation, whichever is less. **Note:** If you are self-employed, you can set up a Keogh plan.

How to Put an IRA to Work for You   Here are some ways to put your IRA to work:

- *Certificates of deposit (CDs).*   If you are conservative, put money in CDs. Returns on CDs are not flashy, but you sleep well at night!

- *Money market funds.*   Again, when you put safety over anything else, you can put your IRA in a money market fund that specializes in Treasury securities.

- *Bond funds and gold funds.*   These offer a way to get income while hedging against inflation.   **Warning:** With any hedge, you reduce risk but at the same time reduce return.

- *Ginnie Maes.*   Many financial advisors recommend Government National Mortgage Association mutual funds. They pay monthly principal and interest.

- *Mutual funds of "blue chip" stocks.*   If you are investment-oriented but want professional management, you can invest in a mutual fund concentrating in large, established companies. Over time, dividends will compound. In case stock prices tumble, think long-term.   **Note:** By the time you retire, many more bull markets will have occurred to boost the value of those shares.

- *Fund of funds.*   When using a family of funds, you pay no sales charge when switching.

- *United States gold and silver coins.*   IRAs can include United States gold and silver coins. They have the potential for future appreciation.

The Basics of Annuities   An annuity is a savings account with an insurance company or other investment company. You make either a lump-sum deposit or periodic payments to the company; at retirement, you "annuitize"—receive regular payments for a specified time period (usually a certain number of years or the rest of your life). All of your payments build up tax-free, and are taxed only when withdrawn at retirement, a time when you are usually in a lower tax bracket.   **Note:** Although mostly sold by life insurance companies, annuities are really the opposite of life insurance: annuities pay off when you retire; life insurance pays off when you die.

Annuities come in two basic varieties: fixed and variable.

- *Fixed-rate annuities.*   In a fixed annuity, the insurance company guarantees your principal plus a minimum rate of interest.   **Tip:** If you have little tolerance for risk, the fixed annuity is an ideal investment.   **Note:** In buying a fixed annuity, you should be aware of two interest rates. One is the minimum guaranteed rate, which applies for the duration of the contract. The other is the "current" rate of interest, which reflects market conditions.

- *Variable annuities.*   With a variable annuity, the company does not provide the same guarantee as with fixed annuities. The company invests in common stocks, corporate bonds, or money market instruments, and the investment value fluctuates with the performance of these investments. **Note:** With a variable annuity, you bear the risk of the investment options. The good thing is that most companies allow you to switch to another fund within the variable type.

Remember: Annuities can be for everybody. For young people, the vehicles are an excellent forced savings plan. For older people, they are tax-favored investments that can guarantee an income for life.

Annuities are not without their pitfalls. Consider these disadvantages before making your final decision.

- Penalties for early withdrawals of money imposed by the IRS and the insurance company
- Surrender charges if you decide to cash in the contract early
- Payments with after-tax dollars for non-qualified annuities

Note: Qualified annuities, on the other hand, are used to fund such vehicles as Individual Retirement Accounts (IRAs) and pension plans. In a qualified annuity, the contributions not only grow tax-free but are also either tax-deductible or not included in your income.

Which should you choose, qualified or nonqualified annuities?

Recommendation: If you are eligible, you should always make contributions to programs like IRAs and pension plans first. It makes sense to invest first in a plan where contributions are made with before-tax dollars.

Don't forget: Unlike pension plans and IRAs, annuities involve no limitations on the amount you may contribute.

How to Purchase Annuities   Here are some tips for buying an annuity:

- Deal with a firm that is financially sound and strong. It's not always obvious which firms are sound: for example, Baldwin-United, a leading annuity seller, filed for bankruptcy.

- Only buy annuities from companies which have an A+ rating (you can find ratings in A.M. Best's publication, *Best's Insurance Reports,* 1988). For example, Equitable Life Insurance Company is financially secure.

- Ask the sales representative about the company's investment performance. Make sure you see written documentation.

- When considering variable annuities, select those that are well diversified.

- Ask the sales representative for a detailed description in the contract of all charges (such as surrender, administrative, mortality and expensive risk, and investment advisory fees). List them and compare different annuities.

- Read the sales literature and the annuity contract closely. For variable annuities, examine the prospectus just as you would for a mutual fund. Companies do not have to issue a prospectus for a fixed annuity, since it is not considered a registered security.

- Shop around. Annuity sellers are very competitive. Comparison shopping will pay off.

How to Check Your Pension Fund

Every year, employees enrolled in hundreds of retirement plans are surprised to find that the "nest egg" they were counting on for their later years is not as secure as they once believed. Employers may have used pension assets to make questionable loans, to make bad investments, or simply to "line their own pockets." **Tip:** Check your pension fund on a regular basis. You do not want to find out at retirement that the fund has been mismanaged. Here are some questions you might want to ask about your pension plan:

- Are your pension plan's investments diversified enough?
- What kind of investments have been made?
- Is there evidence of financial losses or loans in default?
- Have there been suspicious transactions with people that have connections with the fund?
- Do the fees paid to the trustees or managers seem excessive?
- Have CPAs given any "qualified" or negative opinions on the plans?

Warning: Most employer pension plans are built and funded on the assumption that many plan members will never receive benefits. It is important to check out what the rules are as early as possible so you can guard against becoming one of those losers (nonqualifiers). For example, quitting a job a few months—or even weeks or days—before a certain pension deadline might result in a loss of pension rights.

Here are some points to investigate:

- Is your job covered by your company pension plan?
- When will you become eligible for membership?
- How long must you work before your benefits are vested?
- How many hours must you work during the year to remain in the plan and accrue benefits?
- What is the formula for determining your benefits?

- What is the earliest age, or combination of age and years of service, at which you may retire?

- How much will your retirement benefits be reduced if you retire early?

- How much will your retirement check be increased if you stay past age 65?

- Will your pension amount be reduced by Social Security benefits, and if so, by how much?

- What would happen to your pension status if you took a leave of absence?

Conclusion

We all know that for most people Social Security benefits are not sufficient for their retirement needs. Retirement planning is a critical part of your financial plan. It should include consideration of future financial goals and needs as well as a sound savings plan to serve those goals and needs. There are different types of retirement plans: company pension plans, company-sponsored retirement plans, and qualified individual plans, such as IRAs and Keoghs. The sooner you get started, the easier it will be to alter your plans to meet future retirement needs.

Index

About the Authors

JOEL G. SIEGEL, Ph.D., CPA, is currently Professor of Accounting and Finance at Queens College of the City University of New York. Dr. Siegel is a personal financial planning consultant. He was previously employed by Coopers and Lybrand, CPAs and Arthur Andersen, CPAs and has acted as a consultant in financial areas to many organizations, including International Telephone & Telegraph, Person-Wolinsky Associates, and Citicorp.

Dr. Siegel is the author of 22 books and about 150 articles on financial topics. His books have been published by McGraw-Hill, Prentice-Hall, John Wiley, Barron's, and the American Institute of CPAs. He has been published in numerous financial journals, including *Financial Executive, The Financial Analysts Journal,* and *The CPA Journal.*

In 1972 he was the recipient of the Outstanding Educator of America Award. He is listed in *Who's Where Among Writers* and *Who's Who in the World.*

JAE K. SHIM, Ph.D., is Professor of Accounting and Finance at California State University, Long Beach. He received his MBA and Ph.D. degrees from the University of California at Berkeley. He has published over 50 refereed articles in accounting and finance as well as 15 books. Dr. Shim has been, over a period of 13 years, an industrial consultant on financial matters. He was the recipient of the Credit Research Foundation Award.

The book is filled with real-life examples that you can use in computing your personal financial planning and investment choices in dollars and cents. The examples given in the text for some selected areas are given below.

Planning for Retirement

Contribution needed for a specified amount when you retire. *Ex. 2.7, Fig. 11.1*

Amount needed to receive a specified yearly retirement annuity. *Ex. 2.29*

How much better-off will you be with a 401(K) plan? *Ex. 11.1*

Planning for a College Education

Cost of a college education. *Exs. 10.2, 10.3, 10.9*

Money you will need when child enters college. *Ex. 10.4*

Annual deposit needed to provide for college education. *Ex. 10.5*

What interest rate you must earn. *Ex. 10.7*

Is a graduate degree financially worth it? *Ex. 10.8*

Buying or Renting

How much will your house be worth when you are ready to sell it? *Ex. 2.4*

Handling Debt

Real interest rate on a loan. *Exs. 2.10, 2.27, 2.28*

The periodic payment on a loan. *Exs. 2.24, 2.25*

Years to pay off a loan. *Ex. 2.26*

Investing in Stocks

Rate of return on stock investments. *Exs. 4.1, 4.3, 5.8, 5.9, 5.10, 5.27, 5.28, 6.6*